Railway History in Pictures
East Anglia

Peter Swinger

DAVID & CHARLES
Newton Abbot   London   North Pomfret (Vt)

British Library Cataloguing in Publication Data

Swinger, Peter W.
  Railway history in pictures: East Anglia.
  1. Railways – East Anglia – History – Pictorial works
  I. Title
  385′.09426   HE3019.E/

ISBN 0–7153–8205–5

© Peter Swinger, 1983

All rights reserved. No part of this publication may be reproduced, stored in retrieval system, or transmitted, in any form or by any means, electronic, mechanical, photocopying, recording or otherwise, without the prior permission of David & Charles (Publishers) Limited

Photoset in Times by
Northern Phototypesetting Co, Bolton
and printed in Great Britian by
Biddles Ltd, Guildford, Surrey
for David & Charles (Publishers) Limited
Brunel House Newton Abbot Devon

Published in the United States of America
by David & Charles Inc
North Pomfret Vermont 05053 USA

CONTENTS

	Introduction	4
1	Great Eastern motive power	18
2	LNER motive power on the Great Eastern	27
3	British Railways motive power	30
4	Main Lines	33
5	Cross Country	47
6	The Midland & Great Northern Joint Railway	52
7	The London, Tilbury & Southend Railway	64
8	Seaport branches	68
9	Titled trains	71
10	Byways	76
11	The Modern scene	85
12	Preservation	89

INTRODUCTION

East Anglia has always been a sparsely populated area of England. Even by the outbreak of the second world war Norfolk had changed but little in the preceding century. What impact then must the coming of the railways have had on the essentially rural counties of Norfolk, Suffolk, Essex and Cambridgeshire which comprised the area known as East Anglia?

After its incorporation in 1862 from the amalgamation of many smaller railways promoted during the railway mania, the Great Eastern Railway held sway throughout East Anglia, but suffered two thorns in its side. In North Norfolk lay the Midland & Great Northern Joint Railway while in South Essex there was the London, Tilbury & Southend Railway.

The original London terminus for the Eastern Counties Railway was at Shoreditch which soon became inadequate. The Great Eastern opened Liverpool Street station on 2 February 1874, the station being built in something of a dip, lower even than the surrounding City streets, which entailed a steep climb out to Bethnal Green. At this station the main line divides, the line for Cambridge turning to the left while that for Suffolk and Norfolk goes ahead through Essex. About four miles out is Stratford, the site of the locomotive and carriage works of the Great Eastern. It was here on 10 and 11 December 1891 that Class Y14 0–6–0 was erected in the world record time of 9hr 37min for the construction of a steam locomotive. Ahead from Stratford lies Ilford where the flyover built in conjunction with the post second world war electrification served to alleviate the problem of transferring suburban lines from the east side of Liverpool Street over the main lines at Ilford from which point suburban trains run on the north side of the formation until the end of quadruple track at Shenfield. The junction for the Southend line is at Shenfield from whence the main line heads through Chelmsford, the County town of Essex to the junction at Witham where the branch line to Braintree and formerly to Dunmow and Bishops Stortford on the Cambridge line, runs off to the left. This line had been opened by the Great Eastern in 1869 which had taken over the Bishops Stortford, Dunmow & Braintree Railway which had got into difficulties long before completion. It is now lifted beyond Braintree & Bocking but was electrified as recently as 1980 which augers well for the future. Witham was also the junction for the branch to Maldon East which linked via Maldon West with the Southminster line at a junction at Woodham Ferrers but fell victim to the Beeching axe and was finally closed to goods traffic on 18 April 1966 and lifted.

At Kelvedon was the junction for the Kelvedon & Tollesbury Light Railway which is described in Byways. At Marks Tey there is a junction with a branch striking northwards to Long Melford where it made a further junction forking left to form the Cambridge to Colchester cross-country line. The other half of this junction went on to Bury St. Edmunds where it joined the Ipswich and Cambridge Main Line. Of the line from Marks Tey all that stands today is the stretch to Sudbury on which Chappel & Wakes Colne station is the headquarters of the Stour Valley Railway Preservation Society which leases the yard from British Rail and is forming an impressive collection of locomotives and rolling stock. At the time of writing negotiations are in hand to run steam-hauled passenger trains on the line at weekends between the regular dmu services. Chappel was the junction of the Colne Valley & Halstead Railway which ran to Haverhill on the Long Melford to Cambridge line and contrived to remain independent until the grouping in 1923.

Colchester is the junction for Walton-on-the-Naze and Clacton-on-Sea line; there was also a branch to Brightlingsea now lifted beyond the junction at Wivenhoe. The line from Liverpool Street to Colchester and the branch on to Clacton and Walton is electrified at 25kV. To the north of Colchester lies Manningtree, the junction for Parkeston Quay and Harwich, and the Great Eastern's outlet to the Continent which it exploited to the full. Manningtree is blessed with a triangle and is one of the few places left in East Anglia where it is still possible to turn a steam locomotive,

Holden produced his P43 4-2-2 in 1890; aesthetically it was his most attractive design to date. No. 11 is seen at Liverpool Street. (*L&GRP*)

the others being March and Norwich. At Bentley lay the junction for the Hadleigh branch, long since lifted, with its two intermediate stations.

Ipswich is the major junction in Suffolk where the main lines divide for Norwich and Norfolk, and the East Suffolk line. The Norwich line strikes almost due north while the East Suffolk line heads to Westerfield (junction for the Felixstowe branch) and Beccles. This once busy main line is now worked entirely by dmus with the exception of one locomotive-hauled train a day in each direction between Liverpool Street and Lowestoft. Of freight there is very little but threats of singling and even closure have so far been resisted. Between Ipswich and Beccles there were four branches: at Wickham Market (the station was actually in the village of Campsea Ash) lay the junction for the Framlingham branch; Wickham Market also controlled the Snape branch; and Saxmundham was the junction for the Aldeburgh line. But of the four branch lines off the East Suffolk line, one, that to Felixstowe, is still fully operational with hopes of electrification if the catenary ever reaches Ipswich. The Aldeburgh branch is lifted beyond Leiston the section still extant being operational for the movement of spent fuel from the Central Electricity Generating Board's nuclear power station at Sizewell. Halesworth was not a true running junction but was the terminus of the wildly eccentric narrow gauge Southwold Railway.

Beccles was a three-way junction: to the west lay the Waveney Valley line which meandered across to Tivetshall on the Ipswich to Norwich line; to the north was Yarmouth, and to the east Lowestoft. Today only the line to Lowestoft is in existence.

Returning to Ipswich we trace the route to Norwich passing through Claydon, Needham (reopened on 6 December 1971 after earlier closure as Needham Market) and Stowmarket to reach the junction at Haughley. Here the main line divides, the line to Norwich continues in a roughly northerly direction, with the line to Bury St. Edmunds and Cambridge running almost due west. Haughley was also the junction for the Mid-Suffolk Light Railway which was said 'to start from nowhere and end in the middle of a field'. En route to Norwich there was just one short branch at Eye, while Diss was the junction for the goods only branch to Scole. At Tivetshall we meet the closed route from Beccles while at Forncett was a junction with a short branch which struck north west to link with the Ely–Norwich line at Wymondham. Thorpe station was the terminus for the Great Eastern in Norwich and the only station of the original three still open in the City. Thorpe being a terminus it was necessary for the Cromer expresses calling at Norwich to reverse, leaving Norwich on the route towards Yarmouth but branching north at Whitlingham. Just outside Norwich Thorpe was a by-pass line, Wensum curve, which formed a triangle with the London and Yarmouth lines into Thorpe. It was used at

The 'Fifteen hundred' class leader, No 8500 as modified with ACFI feed-water heater. This equipment did little to enhance the appearance of these engines. (L&GRP)

one time by Cromer expresses not calling at Norwich. There were two junctions before Cromer High was reached, at Wroxham where a line ran west to the junction at County School with the route from Wymondham, and at North Walsham where the Norfolk & Suffolk Joint – a concern owned by the GER and M&GN – branched to the right serving a number of small towns on the coast.

From North Norfolk we return to Bethnal Green to trace the route to Cambridge which passes through East Hertfordshire to Bishops Stortford, then Elsenham, junction of the one-time Thaxted tramway, Audley End, Whittlesford and Shelford to Cambridge. Here the London & North Western Railway obtained a foothold in East Anglia with its route from Oxford and Bletchley. Here also the Great Northern was encountered with its branch from Hitchin. And the GE line from Haughley and Bury St Edmunds passing through Newmarket also linked with the Cambridge main line. Slightly north of Cambridge lay Barnwell Junction with branches to St Ives and Mildenhall. The main line continues to Ely from where it strikes almost due north to Kings Lynn. Until the Beeching years it went further to serve the West Norfolk coast at Hunstanton. A junction at Heacham took the line to Wells-next-the-Sea where the line from County School also terminated. From Ely lines branch west to March and Peterborough and east to Thetford and Norwich and still carry traffic from East Anglia to the Midlands and North. Norfolk and Suffolk were liberally criss-crossed by lines as reference to the map will show.

Until the Grouping in 1923, the lines so far mentioned were entirely Great Eastern routes, notwithstanding working agreements, but in North Norfolk ran the Midland & Great Northern Joint Railway. The M&GN was formed on 1 July 1893 by the Midland Railway and the Great Northern to take over the Eastern & Midlands Railway which had itself been formed on 1 January 1883 by an amalgamation of the Lynn & Fakenham, Yarmouth & Norfolk and the Yarmouth Union Railways. On 1 July 1889 the Eastern & Midlands absorbed the Midlands and Eastern which had been constituted on 27 March 1866 from the Norwich & Spalding, Spalding & Bourne and the Lynn & Sutton Bridge Railways. The Peterborough, Wisbech & Sutton Bridge Railway had remained independent from the Midlands & Eastern but came into the Eastern & Midlands fold in 1883. The Midland & Great Northern Railway existed as a separate entity until 1 October 1936 when working was taken over by the London & North Eastern Railway.

To the south of Great Eastern territory lay the London, Tilbury & Southend Railway, promoted by the Eastern Counties Railway and the London & Blackwall Railway. The line had a somewhat chequered career but led a successful 50 year life, during 37 of which it was entirely independent. This line opened in July 1854 and was leased to the

The Thompson rebuild of the B17 as a two-cylinder type designated Class B2. No 1671 *Royal Sovereign* is in workshop grey; as its name implies it was the royal engine. (*L&GRP*)

contractor who built it at a guaranteed return of 6% on the capital of £400,000 plus half the profits, of which there were none. The first trains ran on 13 April 1854 from Bishopsgate (Eastern Counties Railway) and Fenchurch Street (London & Blackwall) joining at Stratford and thence to Tilbury and Southend. It was built to carry Londoners to Tilbury where they could take the ferry to the pleasure gardens at Rosherville near Gravesend on the South bank of the Thames. The London, Tilbury & Southend was among the first lines to add third class coaches to its trains and to abolish second class, and always enjoyed a reasonably healthy goods traffic. The lease was never very advantageous to the Eastern Counties shareholders; while leased the line never owned rolling stock or locomotives, nor was it properly signalled. When the lease expired on 3 July 1875 the directors came to an agreement whereby the Great Eastern would continue to supply the locomotives and coaches, the former for five years the latter for two. This agreement ended on 1 January 1880. By this time the LT&SR had 12 4–4–2 tanks operating to the designs of T. W. Whitelegg, although their design has been variously attributed to him, to their makers Sharpe, Stewart and Co and to W. Adams. Virtually all the railway's locomotives were to be of this wheel arrangement and came to be known as the 'Tilbury Universal Machines'. The first LT&SR coaches were four wheelers of ten tons each. London, Tilbury & Southend independence came to an end on 7 August 1912 when it was taken over by the Midland Railway under an Act of Parliament against strong opposition from the Great Eastern. However, the Great Eastern finally withdrew its opposition agreeing to extend Fenchurch Street, and widen the lines leading to it in prospect of electrification. The Midland agreed to electrify the London, Tilbury & Southend; in exchange the Great Eastern would receive main line running rights by a new loop at Forest Gate from the Colchester line over the Tottenham & Forest Gate line in to St. Pancras. By the same Act the Great Northern received running rights as far as Tilbury. The first world war prevented electrification of the line and after the Grouping times were not propitious to do so. Electrification finally came after the second world war. The Midland worked the line with the Whitelegg locomotives of father and son but with increasing train weight Stanier's taper boiler 2500 Class 4MT 2–6–4Ts were brought for use on the line, working until the end of steam.

The Great Eastern Railway, in common with many major railways created from amalgamations of smaller lines inherited a motley and varied selection of motive power. The first chief mechanical engineer was Robert Sinclair who was in charge at Stratford at the formation of the Great Eastern in 1862, having come to the Eastern Counties Railway from the Caledonian Railway in 1856, remaining in control until 1866. Under Sinclair most of the Great Eastern locomotives were built by outside contractors. He is best remembered for his W Class 2–2–2s which ran to a total of 30 engines, which for 20 years were responsible for hauling the principal expresses on the Great Eastern. Under Sinclair Great Eastern engines were painted pea green with black boiler

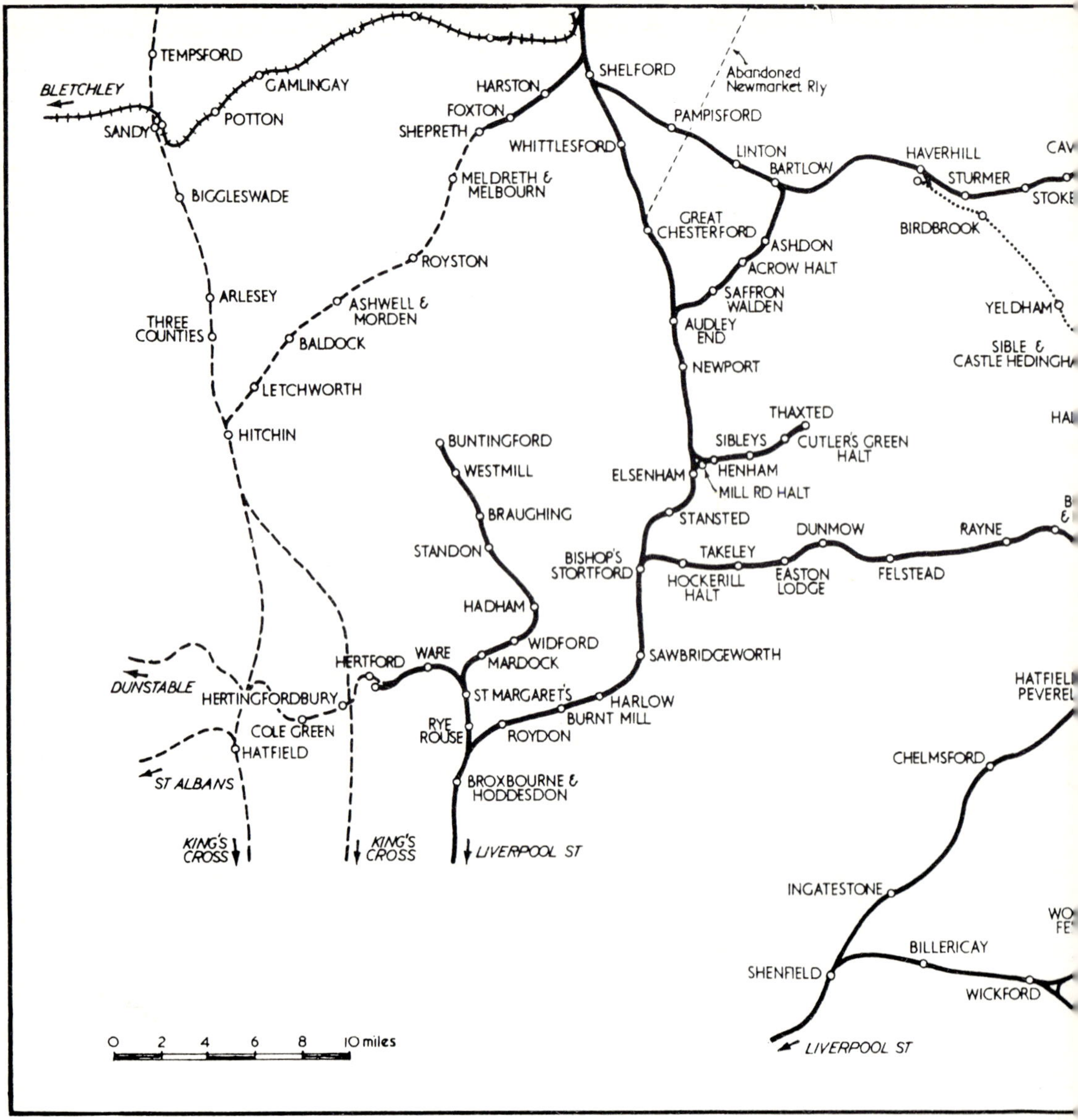

TEMPSFORD
BLETCHLEY
GAMLINGAY
SANDY
POTTON
BIGGLESWADE
ARLESEY
THREE COUNTIES
HITCHIN
LETCHWORTH
BALDOCK
ASHWELL & MORDEN
ROYSTON
MELDRETH & MELBOURN
SHEPRETH
FOXTON
HARSTON
SHELFORD
Abandoned Newmarket Rly
PAMPISFORD
WHITTLESFORD
LINTON
BARTLOW
HAVERHILL
STURMER
BIRDBROOK
GREAT CHESTERFORD
ASHDON
ACROW HALT
SAFFRON WALDEN
AUDLEY END
NEWPORT
YELDHAM
SIBLE & CASTLE HEDINGH
THAXTED
SIBLEYS
CUTLER'S GREEN HALT
HENHAM
ELSENHAM
MILL RD HALT
STANSTED
BUNTINGFORD
WESTMILL
BRAUGHING
STANDON
HADHAM
WIDFORD
MARDOCK
BISHOP'S STORTFORD
TAKELEY
HOCKERILL HALT
EASTON LODGE
DUNMOW
FELSTEAD
RAYNE
SAWBRIDGEWORTH
HERTFORD
WARE
ST MARGARET'S
HARLOW
BURNT MILL
ROYDON
RYE ROUSE
BROXBOURNE & HODDESDON
DUNSTABLE
HERTINGFORDBURY
COLE GREEN
HATFIELD
ST ALBANS
KING'S CROSS
KING'S CROSS
LIVERPOOL ST
CHELMSFORD
INGATESTONE
SHENFIELD
BILLERICAY
WICKFORD
LIVERPOOL ST
0 2 4 6 8 10 miles

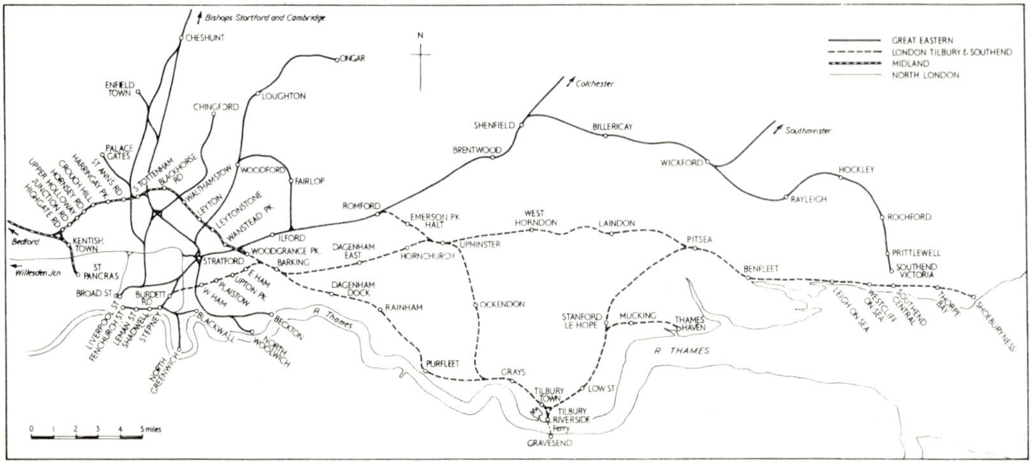

Bishops Stortford and Cambridge
CHESHUNT
ONGAR
N
ENFIELD TOWN
LOUGHTON
CHINGFORD
PALACE GATES
ST ANNS RD
HARRINGAY PK
CROUCH HILL
HORNSEY RD
UPPER HOLLOWAY
JUNCTION RD
HIGHGATE RD
S TOTTENHAM
BLACKHORSE RD
WALTHAMSTOW
WOODFORD
FAIRLOP
LEYTON
LEYTONSTONE
WANSTEAD PK
Bedford
KENTISH TOWN
ST PANCRAS
Willesden Jcn
ILFORD
WOODGRANGE PK.
STRATFORD
BARKING
BROAD ST
BURDETT RD
E HAM
UPTON PK
PLAISTOW
W HAM
LIVERPOOL ST
FENCHURCH ST
LEMAN ST
SHADWELL
STEPNEY
BLACKWALL
NORTH GREENWICH
NORTH WOOLWICH
BECKTON
R Thames
ROMFORD
EMERSON PK HALT
DAGENHAM EAST
HORNCHURCH
UPMINSTER
DAGENHAM DOCK
RAINHAM
OCKENDON
PURFLEET
GRAYS
SHENFIELD
BRENTWOOD
Colchester
BILLERICAY
WICKFORD
Southminster
HOCKLEY
RAYLEIGH
ROCHFORD
WEST HORNDON
LAINDON
PITSEA
PRITTLEWELL
SOUTHEND VICTORIA
BENFLEET
LEIGH ON SEA
WESTCLIFF ON SEA
SOUTHEND CENTRAL
THORPE BAY
SHOEBURYNESS
STANFORD LE HOPE
MUCKING
THAMES HAVEN
R THAMES
TILBURY TOWN
LOW ST
TILBURY RIVERSIDE
Ferry
GRAVESEND
GREAT EASTERN
LONDON TILBURY & SOUTHEND
MIDLAND
NORTH LONDON
0 1 2 3 4 5 miles

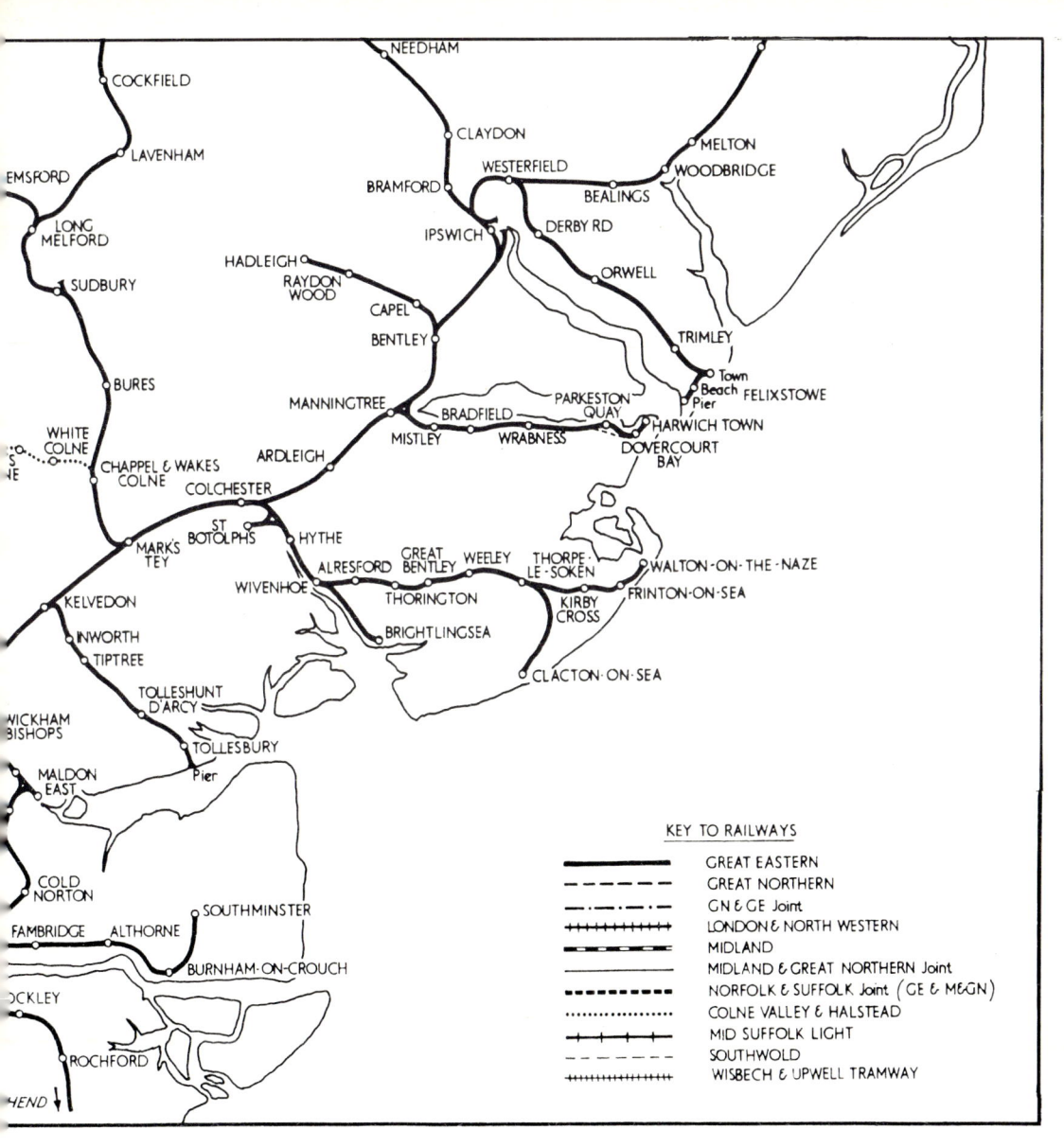

Above: Southern part of East Anglia.
Left: Enlargement of London lines and GE and LTS routes to Southend.

bands and red lining.

In February 1882 Thomas W. Worsdell came to Stratford and is best remembered for making it Great Eastern policy that in future all its locomotives should be built in Stratford; strange to relate, until then Stratford had only built 160 locomotives in its 35 year existence. His first design was a 2–4–0 designated Class G14 which was built in 1882/3. They were attractive locomotives and brought a new style to Stratford with straight splashers over their coupled wheels, but were not very successful. They were followed by the Y14 0–6–0s which by comparison were an outstanding success. Under the LNER they became class J15 and lasted well into BR days. A representative of the class has been preserved by the Midland & Great Northern Preservation Society at Sheringham. It is perhaps ironic that the only working example of a Great Eastern locomotive is now to be seen on M&GN metals! In his short term of $3\frac{1}{2}$ years at Stratford Worsdell had achieved a great deal; under his leadership the Great Eastern adopted the outstanding livery of Royal Blue for locomotives. With this colour scheme came the vermilion buffer beams and coupling rods, gold lettering and cast brass number plates with figures set in relief against a red background.

Following Worsdell, James Holden came to the Great Eastern after spending 20 years at Swindon. Upon his retirement he left behind him locomotives of such rugged designs that many were working half a century after his departure. His first design was the T19 2–4–0 which was to be the mainstay of Great Eastern working for many years and one of which was the first locomotive to work non-stop from Liverpool

Stratford shed on St Valentine's Day 1951, with BR standard Pacific No 70000 *Britannia* itself, shortly after delivery. (*R. C. Riley*)

Street to Cromer. Following an experiment with one of these when the coupling rods were removed, he discovered that the converted locomotive, now effectively a 2–2–2, showed such a clean pair of heels that he embarked upon a class of single driver 2–2–2s which became class D27. In 1890 came Holden's second class of 7ft single driver, the class P43 4–2–2 from the aesthetic point of view, his best design so far. They were not dissimilar in appearance from Johnson's 4–2–2 on the Midland; all were fitted for oil burning though boilers were only pressed to 160 lb of steam. Despite the efforts of P43s on such trains as the Cromer Express, which in later days had grown to a load of 270 tons, the writing was on the wall for the single driver locomotive and the time had come for James Holden to apply a leading bogie to a four coupled engine. 1891 saw the introduction of the T26 2–4–0 tender engine, a mixed traffic class broadly similar to the T19 2–4–0s, the only difference being the driving wheels which were 5ft 8in diameter. The T26s were the most versatile class for which James Holden was responsible, becoming Class E4 under the LNER and lasting almost to the end of steam under BR ownership. An example of the class is preserved at the National Railway Museum as Great Eastern Railway No 490. 1893 saw Holden produce a more powerful class of 2–4–2 tank for intermediate main line work between Liverpool Street, Southend-on-Sea, Witham, Bishops Stortford etc. It had much in common with the E4 2–4–0s previously described; 40 of this class appeared in 1893 to 1895 and a further 10 in 1902.

Classified by the Great Eastern as class E23, all passed into LNER ownership and 15 to BR. The designation was Class F3 under LNER.

In 1900 James Holden's masterpiece emerged from Stratford works. Resplendent in Royal Blue and lined out in scarlet, with brass beading round the rims of the safety valves casing, front and side windows and top and bottom of both Westinghouse brake cylinders, the whole ensemble was topped off with a copper capped chimney. The locomotive was numbered 1900 in honour of the year, and was to be exhibited at the Paris exhibition named *Claud Hamilton* after the chairman of the company. The splashers were cut away to allow access to the coupling rods, which in common with the buffer beams were painted vermilion; the front of the smokebox bore a broad ring of polished steel. Stratford was justly proud of its new express 4–4–0. As Great Eastern numbering had only reached 1119 in 1900 successive Claud's were numbered backwards in batches of 10 every year until 1911, with the exception of 1905. They were originally oil fired, with 7ft driving wheels and were classified S46, D56 and H88 becoming D14, 15 and 16 under LNER ownership. By then they were coal fired. The original 11 built in 1900 had round top tenders and round front cab windows, retained in the 1901 batch, but these had flared top tenders, cabs to the full width of the locomotive and high arched roof, both features which became permanent. The 1902/3 batch were similar but had larger cab front windows conforming to the cab sides and roof and sides of the boiler barrel. 1904 saw a major change in production with the introduction of Belpaire fireboxes on the Clauds while the boiler centre was raised from 8ft 3in to 8ft 5in. James Holden retired in 1907 to be succeeded by his son Stephen Dewar Holden who was in turn succeeded by Alfred J. Hill in 1912. Both continued to build Clauds, the final batch in 1923; two of the last batch were allocated to the Cambridge Royal link and were always immaculate. The whole class eventually received Belpaire fireboxes though only 17 were built in Great Eastern days but between 1923 and 1925 all 121 had received their Belpaires and had been superheated by 1933. It is ironic that all reverted to round top fireboxes under Gresley and Thompson; they also lost their cut away splashers but even in their final condition they were fine locomotives.

By 1909 Stratford had developed a penchant for decorating its locomotives and this appetite spread to the adornment of a class of small 2–4–2 tanks introduced for suburban work. Class Y56 consisted of 12 locomotives built in 1909 and 1910 numbered 1300 to 1311. The entire design was overshadowed by an immense cab having high arched roof and large windows; it was hardly surprising that this diminutive class of locomotive earned itself the soubriquet 'Crystal Palace'. Designated class F7 by the LNER all 12 passed to that railway's ownership, two lasting to BR days being withdrawn in 1948.

1915 saw Alfred Hill introduce a wheel arrangement new to the Great Eastern. This was an 0–6–2 tank for suburban work. Nos 1000 and 1001 were the first two, followed in 1921 by Nos 990 to 999, and 1002 to 1011. As Class L under the Great Eastern they continued to be built by the LNER as Class N7 112 being built from 1925 to 1928. No 999 was the last locomotive to be built at Stratford and has been privately preserved at Chappel & Wakes Colne.

Engineering restrictions on Great Eastern metals had always imposed heavy demands on the design staff at Stratford. Notwithstanding this and before his early retirement in 1912 Stephen Dewar Holden saw the introduction of the Great Eastern's first 4–6–0 express passenger locomotives, designated S69 they had the same adornment as his father's Claud Hamiltons, the entire build passing to LNER ownership and becoming the now famous class B12. The 19in by 26in cylinders of the Clauds were increased to 20in by 28in and the boiler barrel from 4ft 9in to 5ft 1in. Belpaire fireboxes were standard features. The first locomotive in the class was numbered 1500 and they were known coloquially as the 'fifteen hundreds' on the Great Eastern throughout their lives. By 1917 production had reached No 1540; in 1920 a further 20 were ordered from William Beardmore & Co of Glasgow, this being the first occasion since 1884 when a locomotive destined to work on the Great Eastern had been built by an outside contractor. This batch was delivered in 1921 during which year Stratford also produced 1561 to 1570. B12s were also built by the LNER and in 1928 Nos 8571 to 8580 (7000 being added to all Great Eastern numbers) were built by Beyer, Peacock & Co of Manchester. This batch was fitted with oscillating Lentz poppet valve motion. Between 1927 and 1934 55 or the 80 members of the class were provided with ACFI feed water heaters. They looked rather like someone with a pack on their back and earned themselves the soubriquet 'Hikers'. This term was also related to the large cabs, since the fireman had to take a step

The chrome steel smokebox ring and round cab windows are clearly visible in this view of Class D86 1901-build No 1883 descending Brentwood Bank with a Cromer Express in 1901. The leading nine coaches at least are six-wheelers and the whole train is without corridors, since the GE had not yet adopted through gangways generally on main line stock. (L&GRP)

or two from the tender to the firedoor when firing.

At the Grouping the Great Eastern Railway became a constituent part of the London & North Eastern Railway. Herbert Nigel Gresley was the chief mechanical engineer of the Great Northern Railway and was appointed to the same position in the new company. It was clear that some early intake of large motive power would be necessary. In 1914 Gresley had introduced his Class H3 two-cylinder 2–6–0s on the Great Northern Railway which became K2 under LNER ownership; 20 were drafted to the Great Eastern section shortly after Grouping. Gresley's K3 was introduced in 1920 with a similar cab to the K2; when the class was adopted as an LNER standard larger side windows were fitted. The K3 class totalled 193 locomotives all of which passed into BR ownership. The original K3 was a three-cylinder engine which was built as Class K3/2 to the LNER loading gauge and K3/3 which differed only in minor details. Gresley rebuilt a number of Great Eastern designs through his subordinate at Stratford, Edward Thompson; under his direction the B12s were gradually rebuilt, some losing the intricate fretwork beneath the footplating and later all were rebuilt with Gresley round top fireboxes and designated Class B12/3. Happily a member of the class has been preserved by the M&GN Society at Sheringham but at the time of writing is not in working order. Again it is ironic that the ultimate in Great Eastern express passenger locomotives should be preserved on M&GN metals.

As trains became heavier the need for more powerful locomotives became even more evident but the civil engineering restrictions which had bedevilled the Stratford design staff continued. Gresley's answer appeared in 1928 in the shape of a three-cylinder 4–6–0 of unprepossessing yet memorable proportions. The entire class was named, the first one being *Sandringham*, from which they became known universally as 'Sandys'. Not least of the Great Eastern restrictions was the length of the turntables which dictated the use of small tenders, giving the locomotives a somewhat truncated appearance. This was rectified in some of the class in later years by fitting standard LNER tenders when larger turntables were installed throughout the Great Eastern system. The class was designated B17 and a total of 73 engines was built, all of which passed into BR ownership. It is a tragedy that the entire class had been withdrawn before the latter-day preservation of locomotives came about.

Following Gresley's untimely death in 1941 Edward Thompson succeeded to the post of cme and was responsible for two new designs, both of which were used extensively on Great Eastern metals. Yet 1942 was not the best year to embark upon new classes, for supplies were still being directed mainly towards the war effort, but the LNER was in urgent need of a new mixed traffic locomotive. Thompson took the boiler and firebox of the B17, the cylinders of a K2, settled on 6ft driving wheels and thus produced a new engine without the need for retooling. The early examples were named after different breeds of antelope and deer, the fifth one being named *Bongo*. Needless to say it was by that name that the class was often known by enthusiasts. They were built by both LNER and BR, the class finally running to a total of 409 engines. Two have been preserved and can be seen on the Great Central Railway at Loughborough. In 1949, Class L1 saw the light of day, a 2–6–4 tank of very pleasing proportions; it was very versatile and worked over much of the LNER system. They were classified as Class 4MT by BR, a total of 100 being built. Some worked the Felixstowe branch, others the London outer suburban services and on odd occasions they even worked on express services between Liverpool Street and Norwich.

Nationalisation came on 1 January 1948. New motive power plans were laid under the direction of R. A. Riddles for the entire system but the fruits were some three years away and the LNER designs continued to be built. Ever increasing loads necessitated more powerful locomotives which came in the form of the first Standard BR design, the Class 7 Pacifics. But before they had been built three Bullied Battle of Britain light pacifics were loaned to the Great Eastern section by the Southern Region to ease the motive power difficulties. When the Britannia Pacifics came they transformed the Great Eastern section timetables. The first 75min non-stop run from Liverpool Street to Ipswich was made possible with Britannia haulage. With one exception the Great Eastern section enjoyed the final flowering of British passenger steam locomotive power. As the Britannias did much of their finest work in East Anglia it is fitting that both of the preserved examples are based there. The class leader is to be found on the Nene Valley Railway at Wansford, preserved by the Britannia Locomotive Co Ltd, from where it is hoped it will one day head main line steam specials. The other, the official relic, No 70013 *Oliver Cromwell*, which hauled the last official BR steam passenger train in 1968, is housed at Bressingham where on the rare occasions when he is steamed he strides like a caged lion.

In 1958 the first main line diesels came to East Anglia in the form of the 2000hp English Electric 1Co-Co1 type 4s. Subsequently classified as Class 40 their stay on the Great Eastern was not long lived though they are sometimes seen bringing freight trains into Ipswich. The 40s were replaced by the Brush type 4 Co-Co now known as Class 47 which are responsible for hauling the principal main line expresses in company with the English Electric Class 37 Co-Co. One other class of Brush locomotives to be found on Great Eastern metals is the A1A-A1A type 2 and 3 now known as Class 31, which may be seen heading freight trains and secondary services on passenger lines.

Electrification today forms a major part of East Anglian operation. As we have already seen it was discussed for the Tilbury line before the first world war. The Great Eastern thought about it for its intensive London suburban services but instead reorganised its steam operation which for slickness could not be matched anywhere else in the world. Because of the success of the smartly-operated steam workings the LNER deferred plans for electrification which were not raised again until the 1930s, but, delayed by the second world war, did not reach fruition until 1949 with the conversion of the Liverpool Street–Shenfield line to 1500V dc. The Great Eastern route to Southend from Shenfield was electrified on the same system in 1956, and as part of the general British Railways mid-1950s modernisation plan the suburban lines to Enfield, Chingford and Bishops Stortford together with the London, Tilbury & Southend routes were converted to electric working in the early 1960s. But the system had changed and high voltage alternating current was now the new standard, largely at 25kV. However, in the inner suburban areas a lower voltage of 6.25kV was used, to which system the original 1500V dc to Shenfield was converted as part of main line electrification to Colchester, Clacton and Walton-on-Naze. This meant that the trains had to be fitted

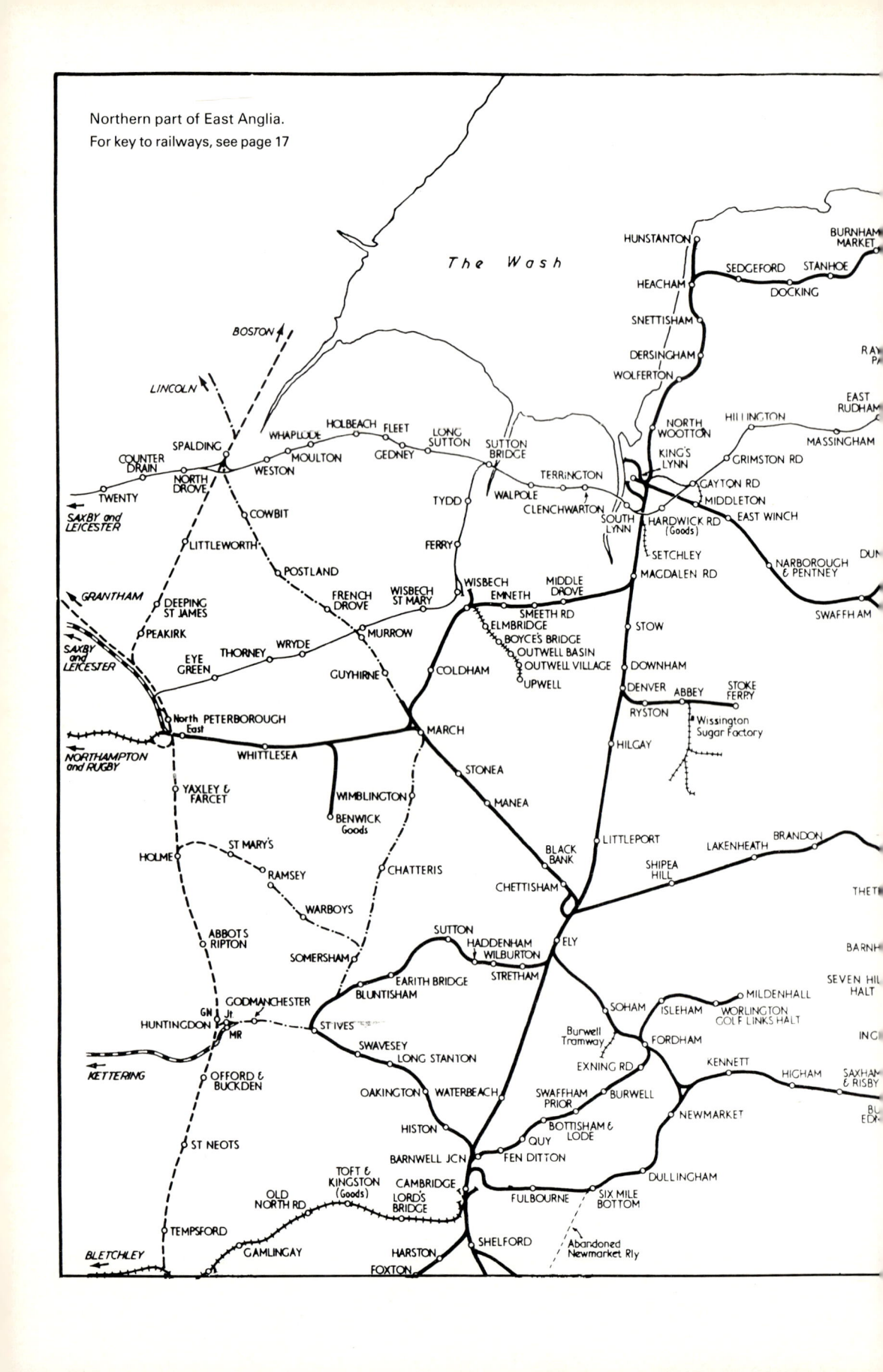

Northern part of East Anglia.
For key to railways, see page 17

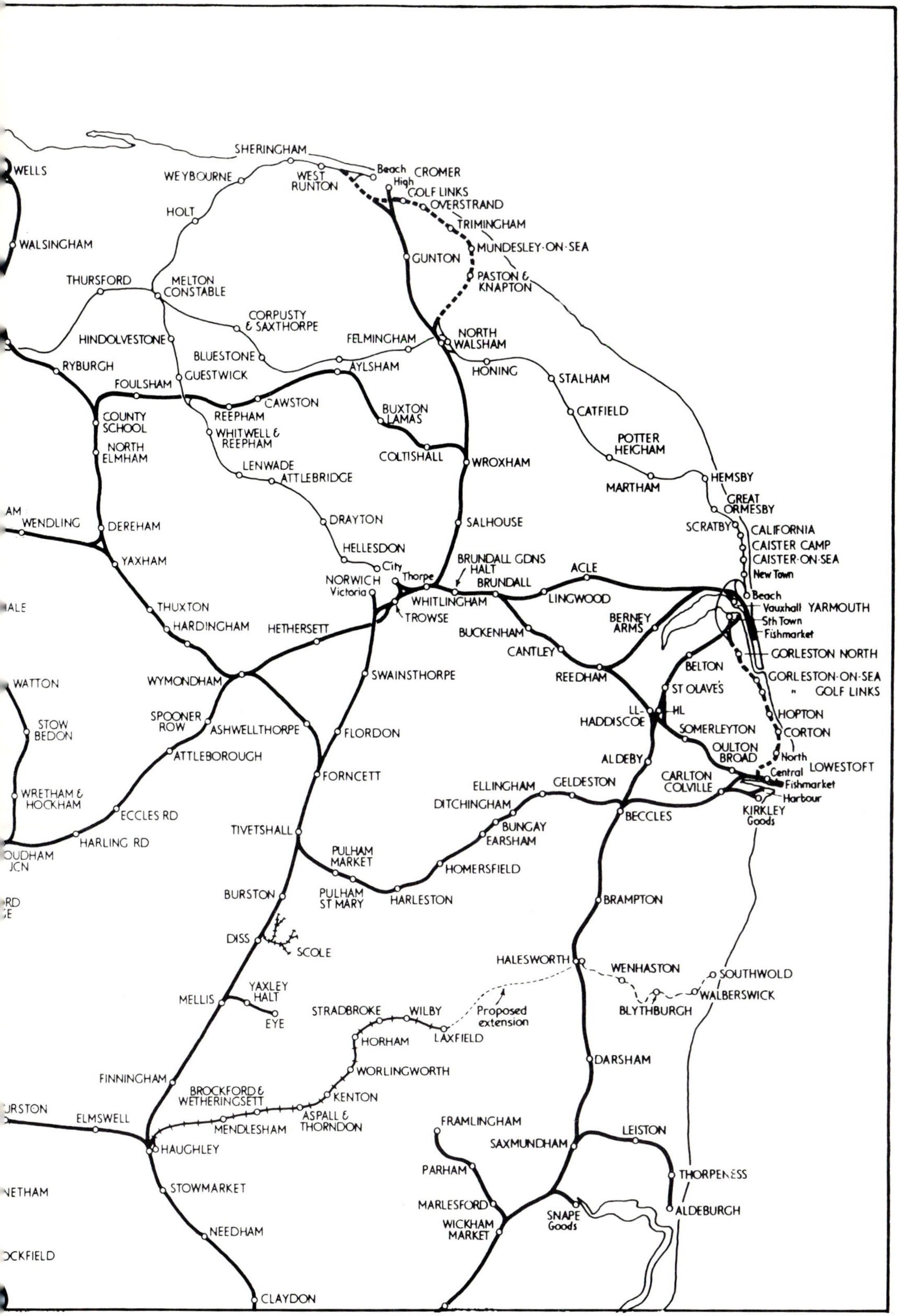
SHERINGHAM
WELLS
WEYBOURNE
WEST RUNTON
Beach
CROMER
High
GOLF LINKS
OVERSTRAND
TRIMINGHAM
HOLT
MUNDESLEY-ON-SEA
WALSINGHAM
GUNTON
PASTON & KNAPTON
THURSFORD
MELTON CONSTABLE
CORPUSTY & SAXTHORPE
HINDOLVESTONE
FELMINGHAM
NORTH WALSHAM
BLUESTONE
RYBURGH
AYLSHAM
HONING
GUESTWICK
STALHAM
FOULSHAM
CAWSTON
REEPHAM
BUXTON LAMAS
CATFIELD
COUNTY SCHOOL
WHITWELL & REEPHAM
POTTER HEIGHAM
NORTH ELMHAM
COLTISHALL
WROXHAM
LENWADE
ATTLEBRIDGE
HEMSBY
MARTHAM
GREAT ORMESBY
WENDLING
DEREHAM
DRAYTON
SALHOUSE
SCRATBY
CALIFORNIA
CAISTER CAMP
HELLESDON
YAXHAM
BRUNDALL GDNS HALT
CAISTER-ON-SEA
City
ACLE
NORWICH
Thorpe
BRUNDALL
New Town
Victoria
WHITLINGHAM
LINGWOOD
Beach
Vauxhall
YARMOUTH
THUXTON
TROWSE
BERNEY ARMS
Sth Town
HARDINGHAM
HETHERSETT
BUCKENHAM
Fishmarket
CANTLEY
GORLESTON NORTH
BELTON
WATTON
WYMONDHAM
SWAINSTHORPE
REEDHAM
GORLESTON-ON-SEA
" GOLF LINKS
ST OLAVE'S
LL
HL
SPOONER ROW
HADDISCOE
HOPTON
STOW BEDON
ASHWELLTHORPE
FLORDON
SOMERLEYTON
CORTON
ATTLEBOROUGH
OULTON BROAD
ALDEBY
North
LOWESTOFT
FORNCETT
CARLTON COLVILLE
Central
WRETHAM & HOCKHAM
ELLINGHAM
GELDESTON
Fishmarket
Harbour
DITCHINGHAM
ECCLES RD
KIRKLEY Goods
BECCLES
BUNGAY
TIVETSHALL
EARSHAM
HARLING RD
PULHAM MARKET
HOMERSFIELD
BURSTON
PULHAM ST MARY
HARLESTON
BRAMPTON
DISS
SCOLE
HALESWORTH
WENHASTON
SOUTHWOLD
YAXLEY HALT
MELLIS
WALBERSWICK
EYE
STRADBROKE
WILBY
Proposed extension
BLYTHBURGH
LAXFIELD
HORHAM
DARSHAM
WORLINGWORTH
FINNINGHAM
BROCKFORD & WETHERINGSETT
KENTON
ELMSWELL
ASPALL & THORNDON
MENDLESHAM
FRAMLINGHAM
LEISTON
HAUGHLEY
SAXMUNDHAM
PARHAM
THORPENESS
STOWMARKET
MARLESFORD
SNAPE Goods
ALDEBURGH
WICKHAM MARKET
NEEDHAM
CLAYDON

English Electric Class 37 diesel No 37103 speeds through Ilford with the 09.40 Liverpool Street–Harwich Day Continental on 25 June 1980. Although this ought to be a prestige train providing the British end of important continental connections the coaches are Mk 1 and early Mk 2 around 15 years or more old. (*M. L. Rogers*)

for dual voltage. In more recent years the low voltage sections have been converted and the whole network is now at 25kV. Since then the branch from Witham to Braintree has been electrified and plans are well advanced for extension of electrification along the Norwich main line from Colchester to Ipswich and from Bishops Stortford to Cambridge.

All the electric services are worked by multiple units, including some main line corridor sets originally designed for 100mph operation on Clacton/Walton–Liverpool Street services.

East Anglia was blessed with its fair share of titled trains under both the Great Eastern and LNER many of which continued under British Railways, but under the modernisation plan disappeared when naming went out of fashion on BR. The Great Eastern railway richly deserved the 'Great' in its title and not least for its Continental services where its highest level of achievement was reached. No less than five titled trains ran at various times over Great Eastern metals from Liverpool Street to Parkeston Quay where the unquestionable zenith was the train which came to be known as the 'Hook Continental'. The fleet of small liners operated by the Great Eastern Railway from Parkeston Quay to the Hook of Holland formed the gateway to North Germany and beyond. Three complete sets of special coaches were built in 1904, 1924 and 1936 to work the 'Hook Continental'.

The Great Eastern also ran the 'Antwerp Continental'. Sailing via Antwerp afforded the passenger the opportunity to dine at the start of the journey and breakfast at the end of his trip from Parkeston as the ship sailed in the smooth stretch along the River Scheldt. It was initially a summer only train, the set being used on the Clacton service at other times. In later LNER days catering on the 'Antwerp Continental' was handled by the Pullman Car Co which provided three cars for the service. 1927 saw the Zealand Shipping Co reroute its British sailings to Parkeston Quay. Flushing being the home of the shipping line, the LNER not unnaturally introduced a train to coincide with the sailings, which bore the title 'Flushing Continental' and was composed of LNER stock plus a Pullman restaurant car and a first class Pullman. A fifth continental service ran to connect with sailings from Esbjerg on the west side of Jutland in Denmark. Named 'The Scandinavian' it was a summer only train, passengers for the boat in winter having to be content with a section on the rear of the 15.10 for Yarmouth from Liverpool Street which was detached at Manningtree and taken forward to Parkeston. However in summer it blossomed in its own right with Pullman cars. In Coronation year 1937 the LNER decided to extend the steamlined era from the East Coast Main Line to East Anglia. To this end a new six-coach train was built. Two of the B17s were streamlined in the idiom of the A4s and named *East Anglian* and *City of London*. The new train was to be called the East Anglian but the initial schedule hardly justified the euphoria, for the down train ran to a schedule of no more than 51½mph. Consequently it was decided that no supplementary fare could be justified. It was genuinely felt that with a six-coach train hauled by a streamlined 4–6–0 a journey time of two hours should have been possible. October 1948 saw the East Anglian being joined in the timetable by a new express bearing the name The Norfolkman. In the summer the train also ran to Cromer. The Norfolkman was normally loaded to eight coaches worked by a B1.

The summer of 1950 saw two new titled trains running out of Liverpool Street, one on the route of the East Anglian and The Norfolkman and one breaking new ground, the latter unique in that it did not stop at Ipswich. The Broadsman ran on the route of the East Anglian and The Norfolkman. The other titled train introduced in 1950 was the only one to run over the East Suffolk main line on a regular basis. Entitled The Easterling it was a summer only train but had the distinction of running non-stop from Liverpool Street to Beccles; here the train divided running forward to Yarmouth and Lowestoft.

We have seen that Pullman cars made regular appearances on Parkeston Quay boat trains but during the period from the Grouping until the outbreak of the second world war a train of eight Pullmans of both eight- and twelve-wheel types, weighing about 320 tons, was assembled to run from Liverpool Street to Newmarket in connection with the race-meetings. When not being used for this purpose, which was not all that frequent, the LNER had the bright idea of running the set to coastal resorts under the title the Eastern Belle Pullman Limited for which a supplementary fare was charged. Destinations changed daily. It was not unknown for passengers to spend a week's holiday aboard the train returning home each evening to sleep. And what could have been nicer, for restaurant facilities were provided enabling passengers to have breakfast on the down train and dine on the up. Motive power was usually a B12 or B17. Sadly the Belle did not reappear after the second world war. The Fenman was another post-war named train, running via Cambridge to the North Norfolk coast, but to a not very exciting schedule.

In Jubilee year 1977 a train ran for about a month carrying the title The Jubilee and in the summer of 1980 the title The East Anglian was reinstated into the timetables, hauled by a Class 47, leaving Liverpool Street at 16.20 and due into Ipswich at 17.25 with a similarly exciting schedule for the up run from Norwich Thorpe.

As for the railway future in East Anglia, one needs a crystal ball to see what might be intentions of the Government paymasters. There could be more electrification on the main lines if present plans are carried through, but equally there could be further closures of secondary and branch lines which would leave little more than the bare spine main lines to Norwich and Cambridge and possibly the east-west link via Ely to the Midlands in the north of the area, the suburban network in the south, and regrettably nothing much in between.

ACKNOWLEDGEMENTS

The basis of this book is a collection of glass negatives which I obtained some years ago; subsequently I suggested the idea of an album of photographs of the railways of East Anglia (a very neglected area) to Geoffrey Kichenside and it was his suggestion that it should take the format here presented. I am grateful to him and to David & Charles for keeping faith during the book's long gestation period. I would also like to record my thanks to Geoffrey Cordy for producing the prints for me often at very short notice. To my wife Kay I am unbelievably grateful for putting up with countless photographs spread across the lounge floor and producing the final typescript from notes which must have been totally meaningless to her. I believe she now knows more than a little about the railways of East Anglia. Finally, a word of thanks to various friends for the loan of their photographs.

Peter Swinger.

1. GREAT EASTERN MOTIVE POWER

Robert Sinclair's W class 2–2–2 built from 1862 to 1867, in four batches from Fairbairn & Co of Manchester, Slaughter, Gruning & Co, Kitson & Co and the French firm Schneider et Cie of Le Creusot, to haul the principal Great Eastern expresses; here an example is seen in original condition. In their heyday they were divided between the crack crews at Stratford, Cambridge, Ipswich and Norwich, the last working to 1894. (L&GRP)

Probably the first class of 2–4–2T in the United Kingdom, Sinclair's oddly attenuated locomotives earned themselves the soubriquet 'Scotchmen' since they were built by Neilson, Reid & Co of Glasgow. (L&GRP)

T. W. Worsdell's G14 2-4-0 was his first design for the GER. They had a hinged number plate which gave partial access to the driving wheels.

In 1883 Worsdell produced his Y14 0-6-0 which became the ubiquitious LNER J15; No 7814 passes Melton Meadows on the East Suffolk main line with a mixed goods train in 1935.

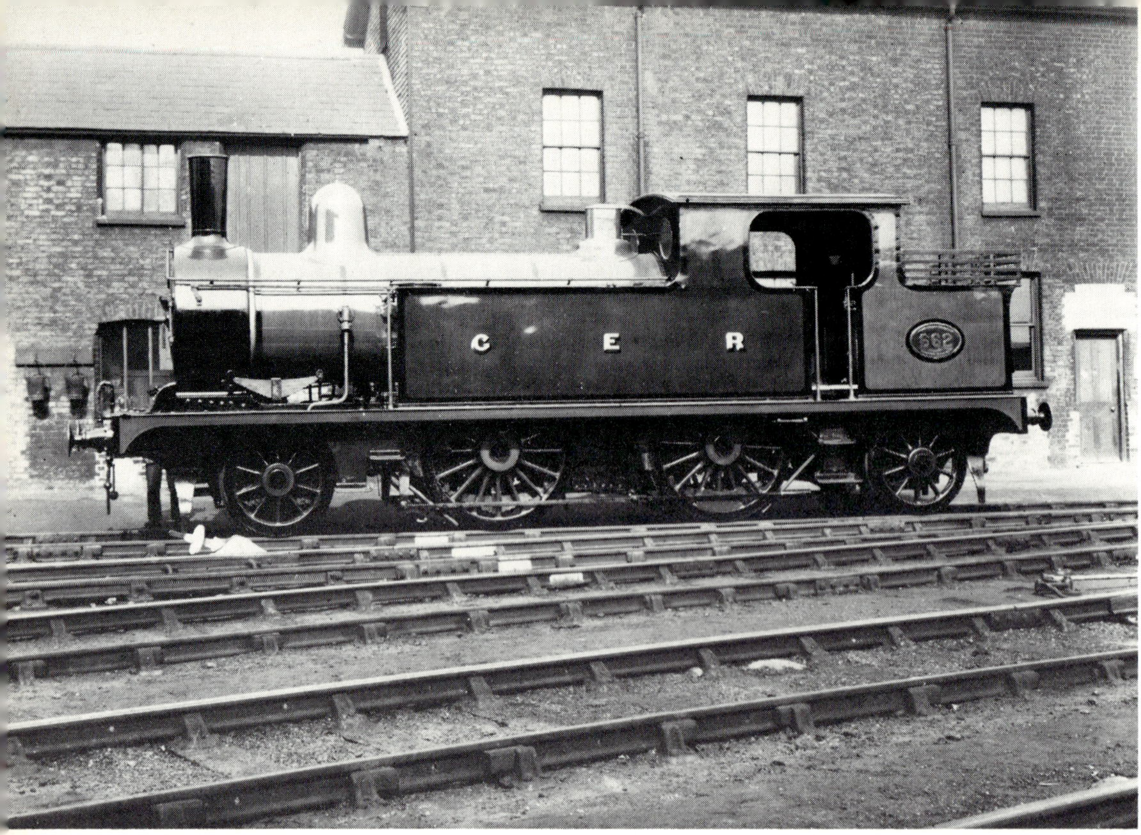
C E R

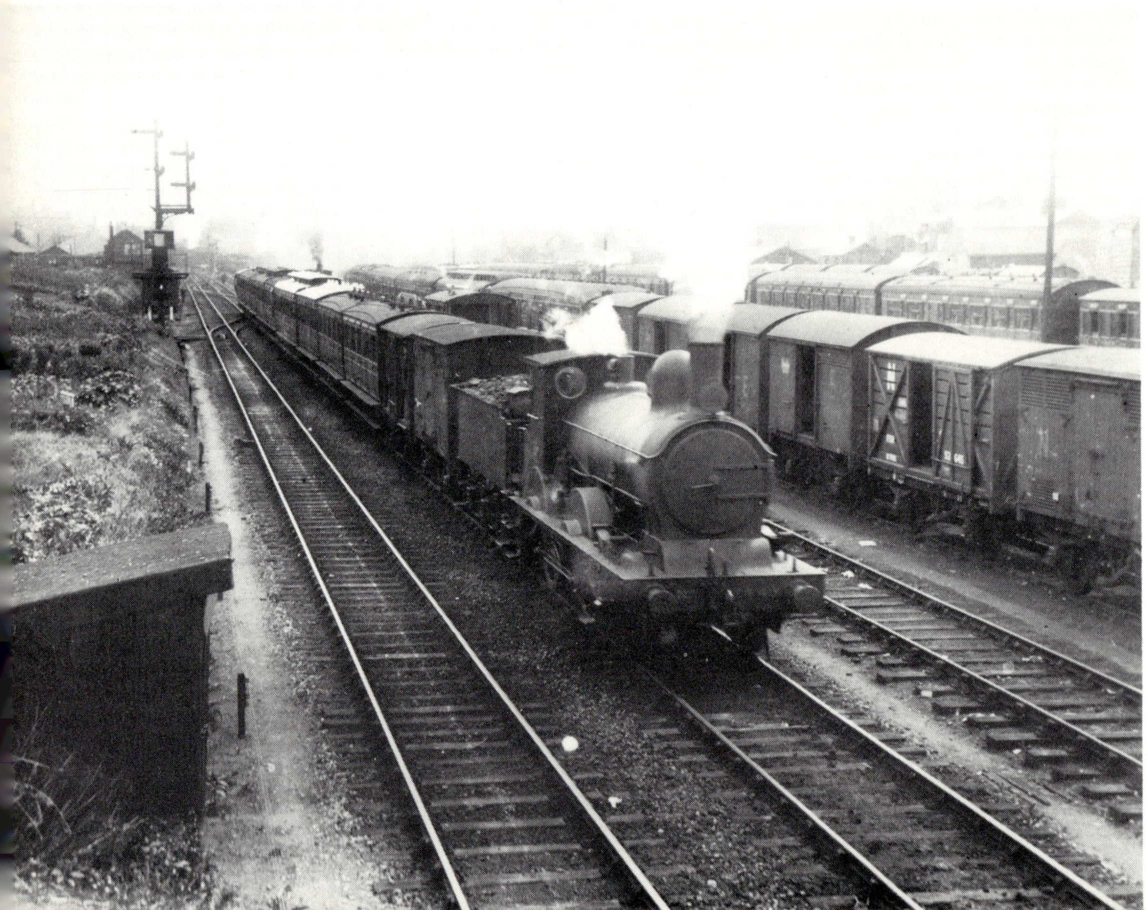

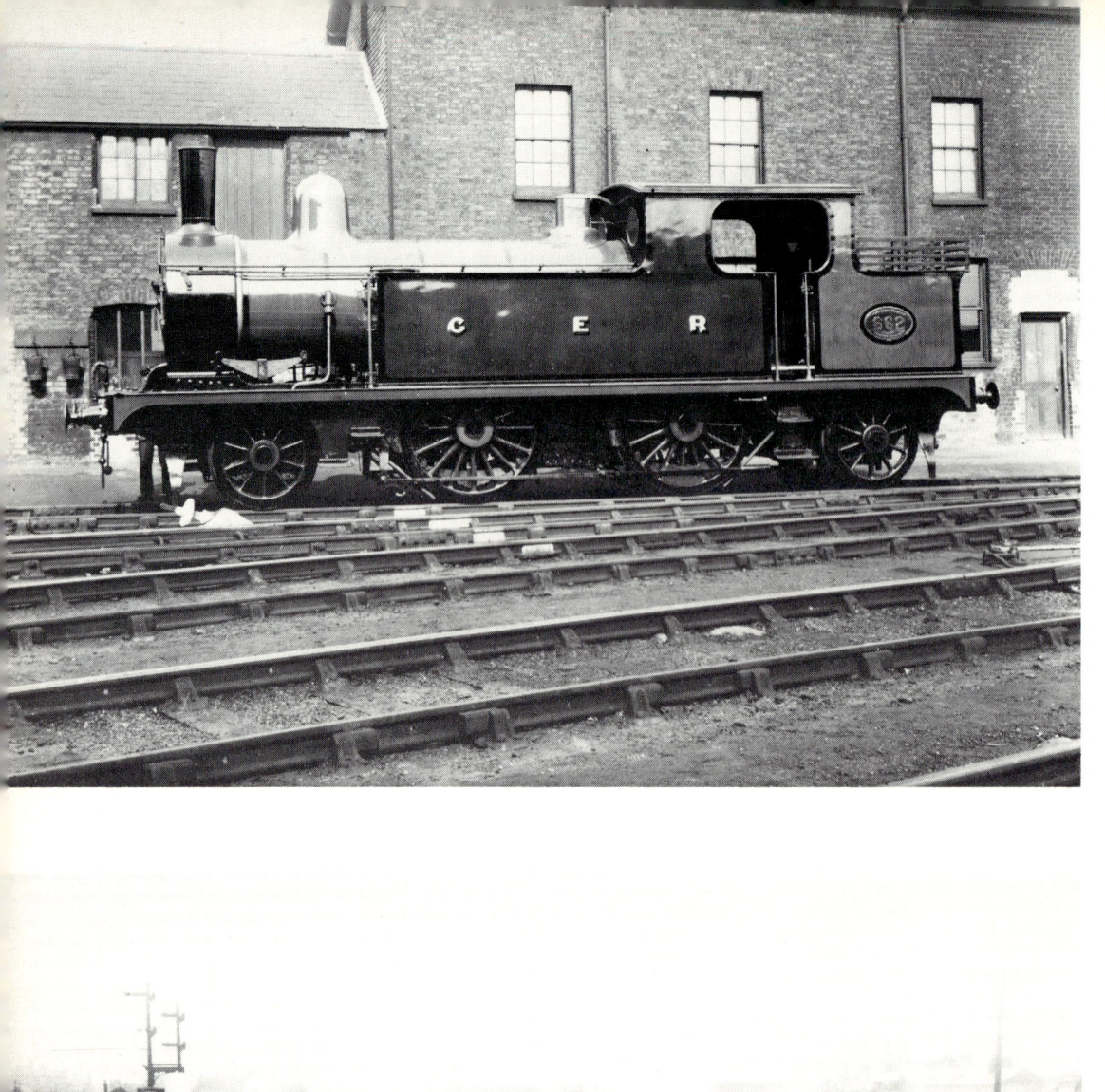

Top left: Worsdell's M15 2–4–2T were equipped with Joy valve gear which may have shown doubtful wisdom for the locomotives had such an appetite for coal that they became known as 'Gobblers', which became a nickname for all GER 2–4–2T.

Above: James Holden's first design at Stratford was his Class T19 2–4–0: about 1900 D27 2–2–2 No 1009, converted for oil firing, and an unidentified T19 are seen on Bentley troughs. (*L&GRP*)

Left: 1891 saw the introduction of the T26 2–4–0 mixed traffic engines which became LNER Class E4, many lasting to BR ownership. In 1926 No 7483 is seen leaving Lowestoft with a very mixed passenger train.

In 1893 Holden produced a more powerful 2–4–2T of Class C32, a total of 50 being built down to 1902 for intermediate main lines. All passed to LNER ownership where they became F3. No 8067 is seen at Clacton-on-Sea in April 1928; 15 of the class survived until Nationalisation.

The original *Claud Hamilton* as built, showing the cutaway splashers allowing access to the coupling rods. (*L&GRP*)

On Saturday 16 June 1928 the 4pm train from Woodbridge was in the charge of No 8873 built in 1902 and No 8807 of 1910. This view clearly shows the larger cab windows and both the round rop and Belpaire fireboxes.

In LNER days No 8787 of the Royal Link is resplendent in apple green at Cambridge on 19 January 1935.

24

Left: The Great Eastern operated one of the most intensive suburban services in the world, all with steam traction. Proposals for electrification did not reach fruition until British Railways days. The Great Eastern even reorganised its steam suburban services at the end of the first world war to standards which could not be beaten for operating slickness anywhere in the world. They acquired the nickname 'jazz trains'. A suburban train approaches Gidea Park headed by 'Crystal Palace' 2–4–2T No 68 just before the Grouping. The coaches started life as four-wheelers. Later they were mounted in pairs on bogie underframes. Some had been widened from 8ft to 9ft as well. (*L&GRP*)

Bottom left: During Hill's tenure the GE introduced a powerful 0–6–2T for suburban work, later classified N7 by the LNER. No 987 is seen here soon after the Grouping. (*L&GRP*)

A more detailed look at a GE class Y56 2–4–2T which later became LNER F7. It is clear from this view why they became known as 'Crystal Palaces'. (*R.J.W. Ind*)

One of S. D. Holden's S69 4–6–0s in original condition at Ipswich in early LNER days when the running number was carried on the tender. Note the intricate cutaways in the splashers reminiscent of his father's Claud Hamilton 4–4–0s. By now they were designated B12.

The final condition of the B12s with round topped firebox. No 61572 takes water in 1958 while Brush Type 2 No D5528 waits to leave with a train for Cambridge. No 61572 was the last B12 to remain in service and has been privately preserved: it is housed on the North Norfolk Railway at Sheringham. (*H. N. James*)

On an August afternoon in 1954 Class K3/3 2-6-0 No 61886 starts a semi-fast for Lowestoft out of Woodbridge.

2. LNER MOTIVE POWER ON THE GREAT EASTERN

On a summer afternoon in 1934 Gresley B17 4-6-0 No 2830 (later named *Tottenham Hotspur*), with the small tender imposed by the short turntables on the Great Eastern, lifts an express from Lowestoft through Woodbridge. The class was renumbered in 1946 into the 1600 series. Immediately behind the tender is a new Gresley teak coach.

Above: Edward Thompson was responsible for two new designs which saw extensive use on the Great Eastern section. In 1945 the L1 class 2–6–4T saw the light of day. In 1958 No 67706 slows at Felixstowe Town signalbox to collect the token for the single line section of the branch as it heads for Ipswich. (*H. N. James*)

Top right: On Ipswich troughs in 1937 streamlined B17 4–6–0 No 2870 *City of London* heads the up East Anglian. (*Dr Ian C. Allen*)

Right: In the summer of 1952 Class B1 4–6–0 No 61235 slows for Westerfield Junction with the Holiday Camps Express for Felixstowe. (*H. N. James*)

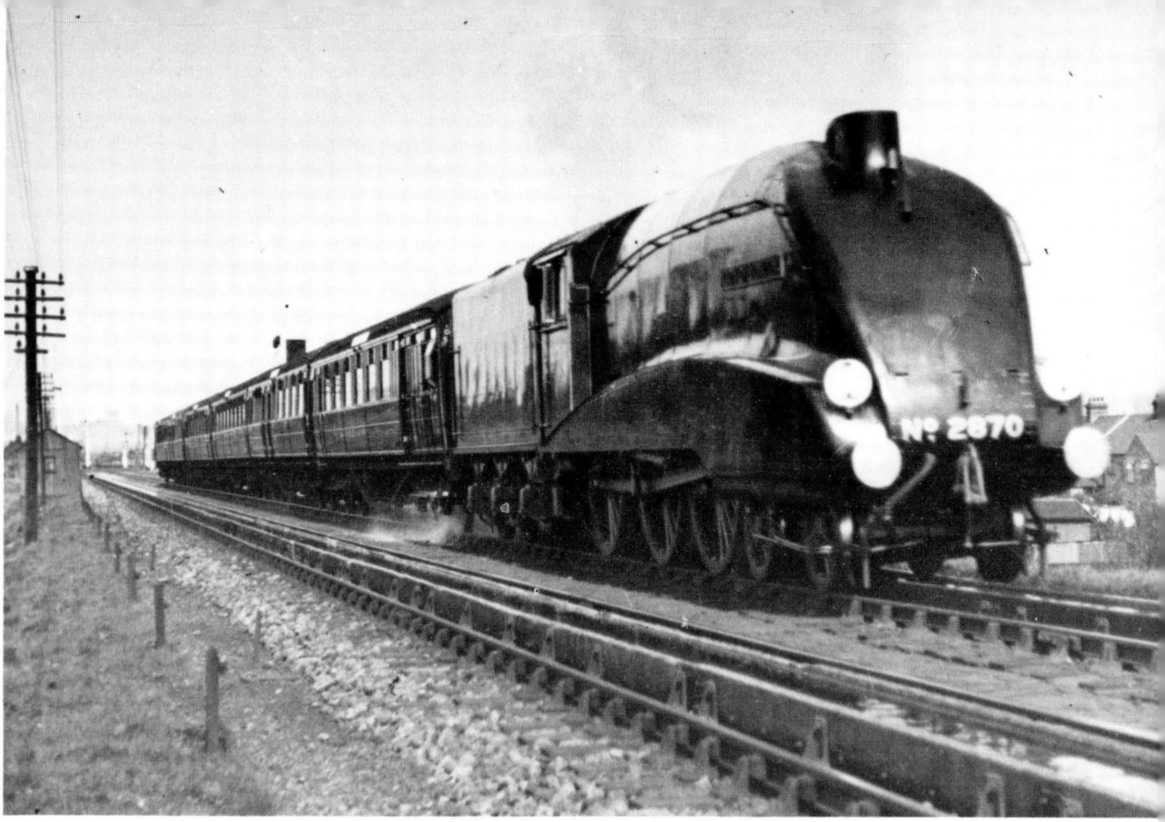
Nº 2870

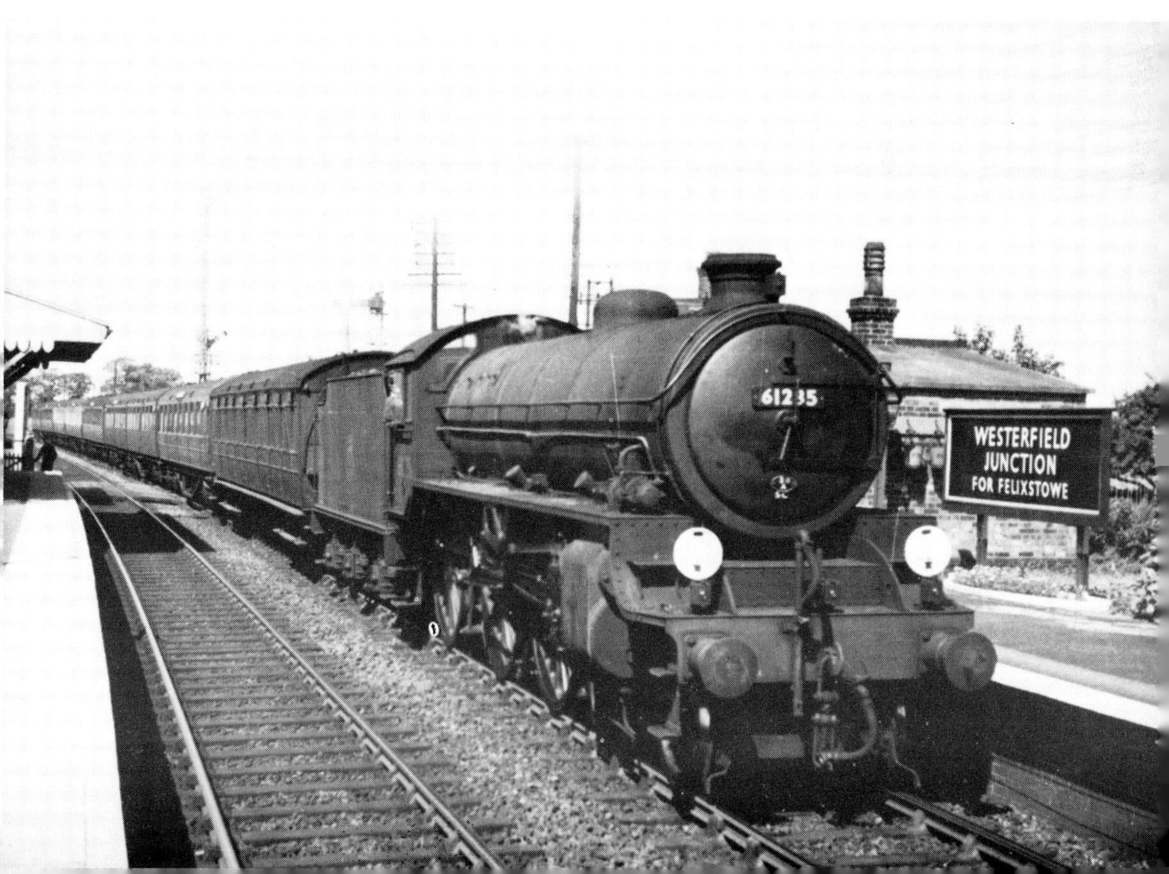
61235
WESTERFIELD
JUNCTION
FOR FELIXSTOWE

In the late 1950s the Eastern Region in common with most other Regions of BR restored the odd locomotive to its original livery. Liverpool Street pilot Class J69/1 0–6–0T No 68619 was returned to Great Eastern blue livery and is seen here in company of two Britannia Pacifics Nos 70010 *Owen Glendower* and 70002 *Geoffrey Chaucer*. (*M. P. Beckett*)

3. BRITISH RAILWAYS MOTIVE POWER

Ipswich Shed on 21 October 1951. Ex-Southern Railway Battle of Britain light Pacific No 34057 *Biggin Hill* is turned during its period of loan from the Southern Region. (*H. N. James*)

The end of steam is in sight on Great Eastern metals. The English Electric 1Co-Co1 type 4s were the first main line diesels to come to East Anglia in 1958. This is the class leader No D200 with the return leg of the inaugural run. The headboard reads 'First 2000hp diesel London to Norwich – Progress by Great Eastern'. Some might question those last four words!

The Brush Class 31 A1A-A1As are currently responsible for freight and parcels and secondary passenger trains throughout East Anglia. Here we see 31268 entering Ipswich with the afternoon down parcels.

Introduced in 1962 the Brush Class 47 Co-Cos are currently responsible for main line expresses to Norwich. On 23 June 1980 No 47184 waits at Liverpool Street to take a down train to Norwich. (*M. L. Rogers*)

During their lifetime just one Deltic worked the East Suffolk main line when in September 1977 No 55015 *Tulyar* brought a special into the area which reversed at Ipswich.

Above: Almost at the end of steam on Liverpool Street suburban services Class N7 0–6–2T No 69671 waits to leave Liverpool Street with a North East London train in April 1961. The coaches are Gresley five-car articulated units known as quint-arts, built in the 1920s for GE service. These trains were the last steam services to retain Westinghouse brakes on mainland BR (the others were on the Isle of Wight). (*John Goss*)

4. MAIN LINES

Overleaf: In 1901 T19 2–4–0 No 735 pilots an unidentified oil burning Claud Hamilton near Brentwood with a down Yarmouth express.

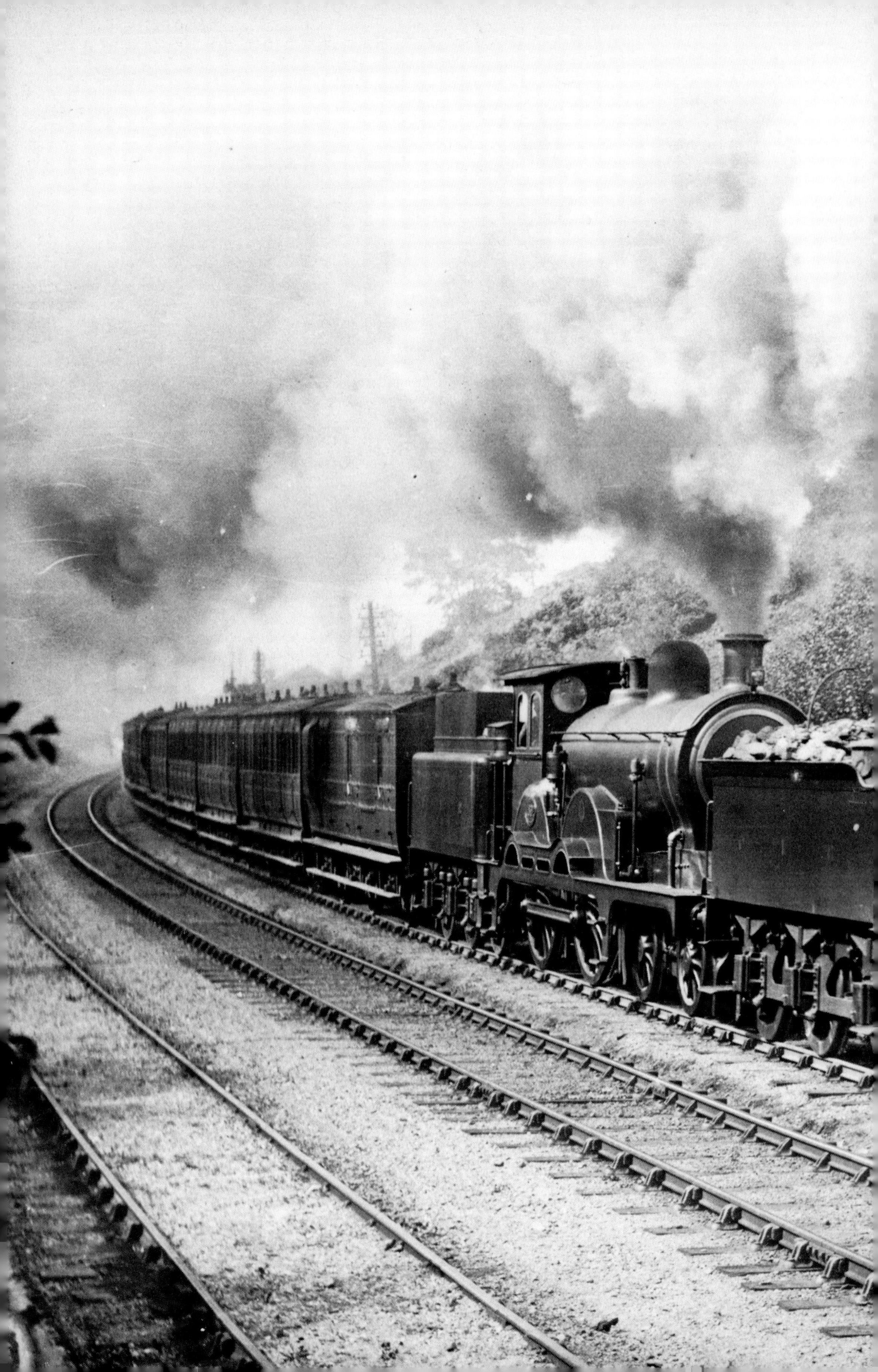

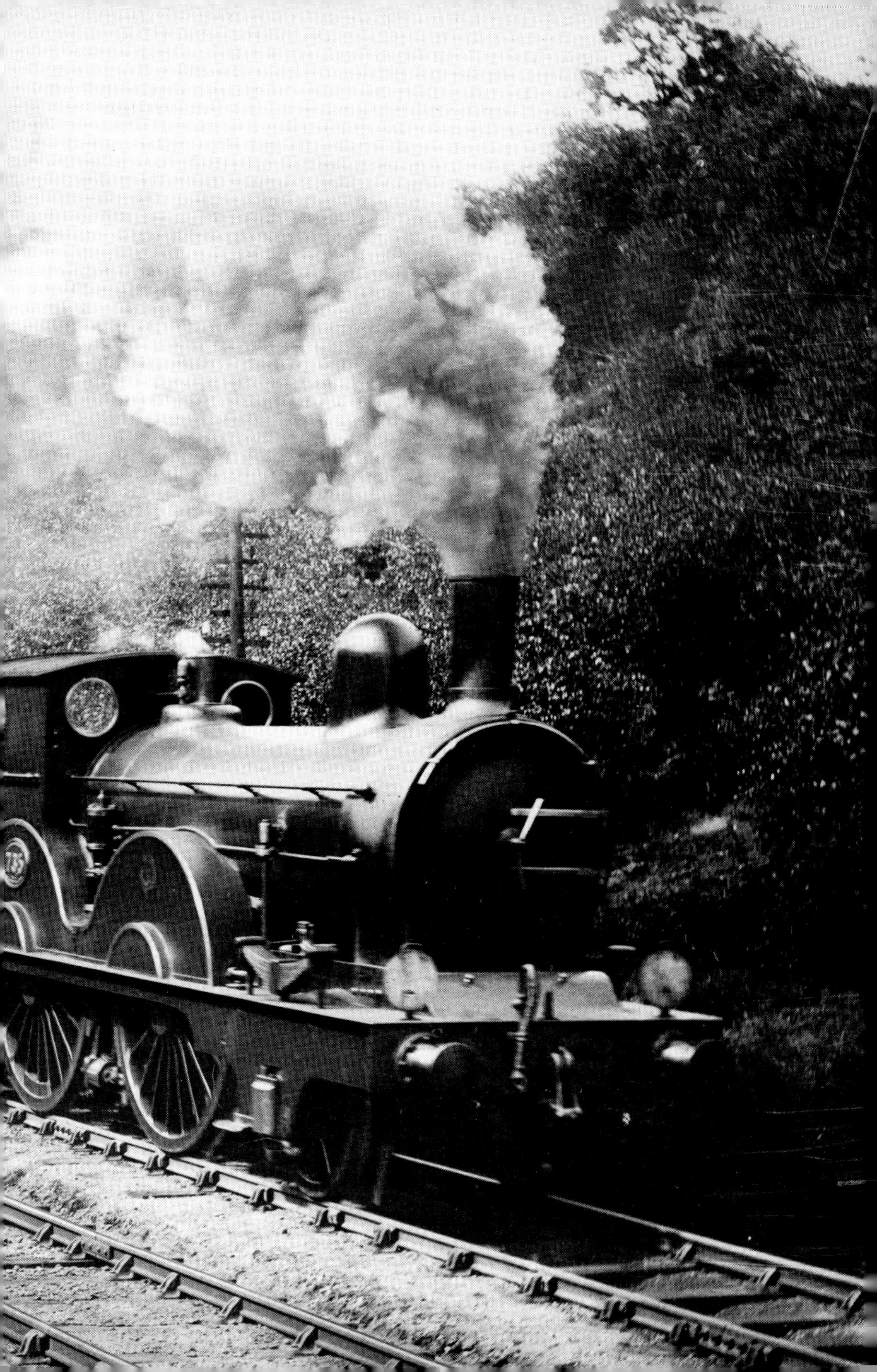

Right: Brentwood Bank in the 1950s with Class B17 4–6–0 No 61601 *Holkham* heading a Clacton Interval Express on the climb towards Shenfield. Behind, a suburban electric train stands in the reversing siding. (*C. R. L. Coles*)

Bottom right: At Shenfield the line departs for Southend; in LNER days Class D16 4–4–0 No 8782 nears Billericay with a down train.

Below: Colchester steam shed was to the north of the station and parallel to the down line. The T19s were rebuilt as 4–4–0s and later designated D13 by the LNER; on 22 April 1929 No 7739 and Neilson-built Y5 0–4–0T are seen on shed. The latter was a Great Eastern design, Class 209, known as 'Coffee Pots'.

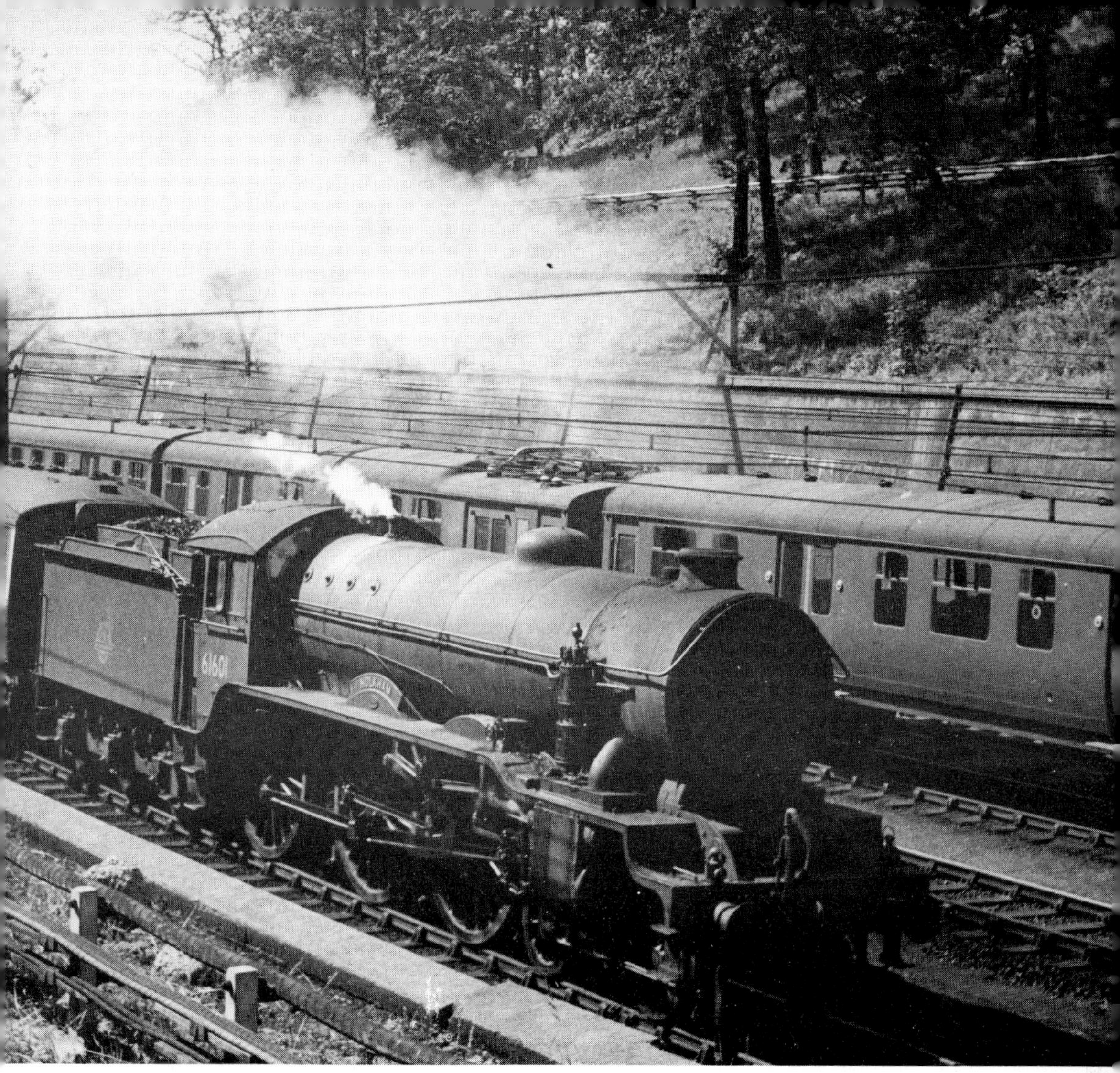
61601

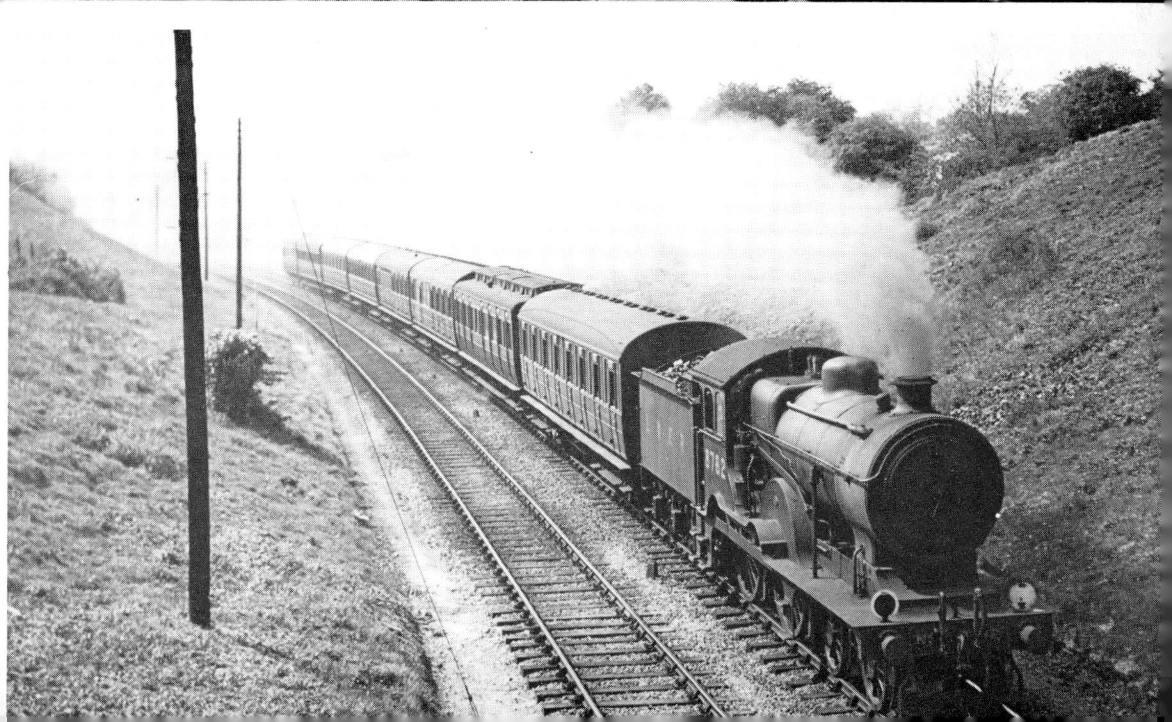

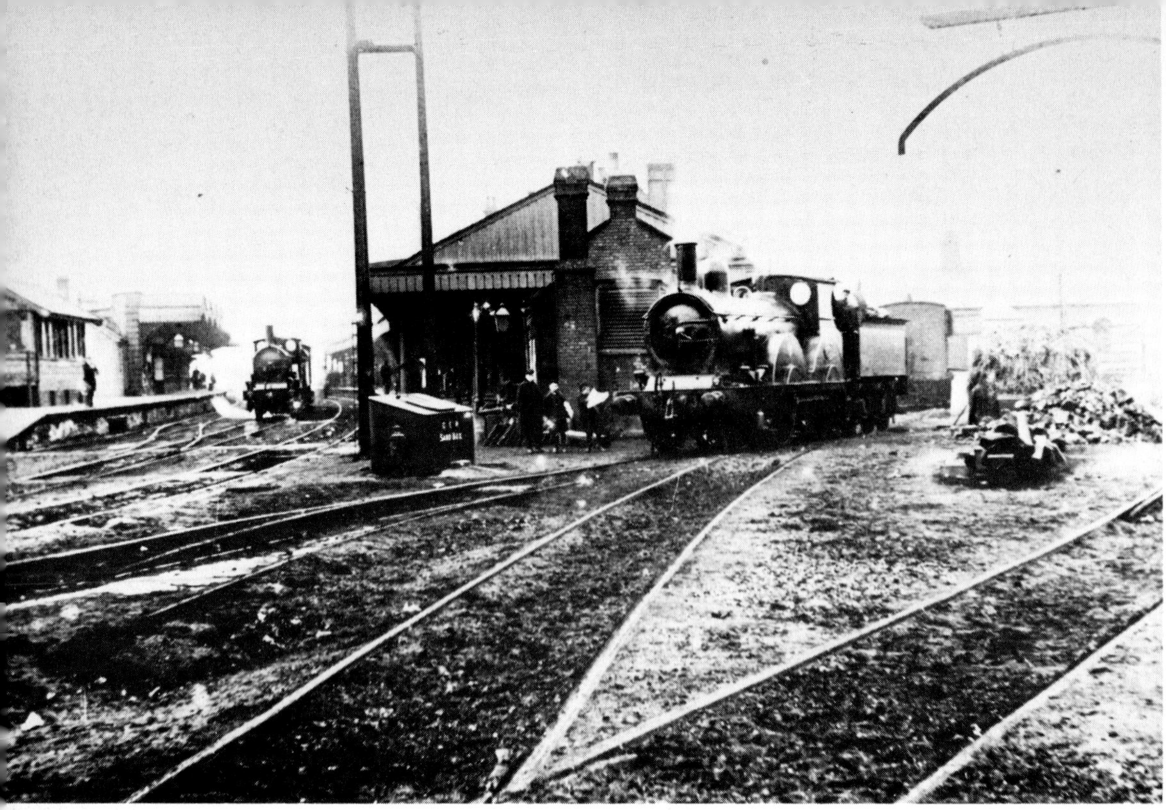

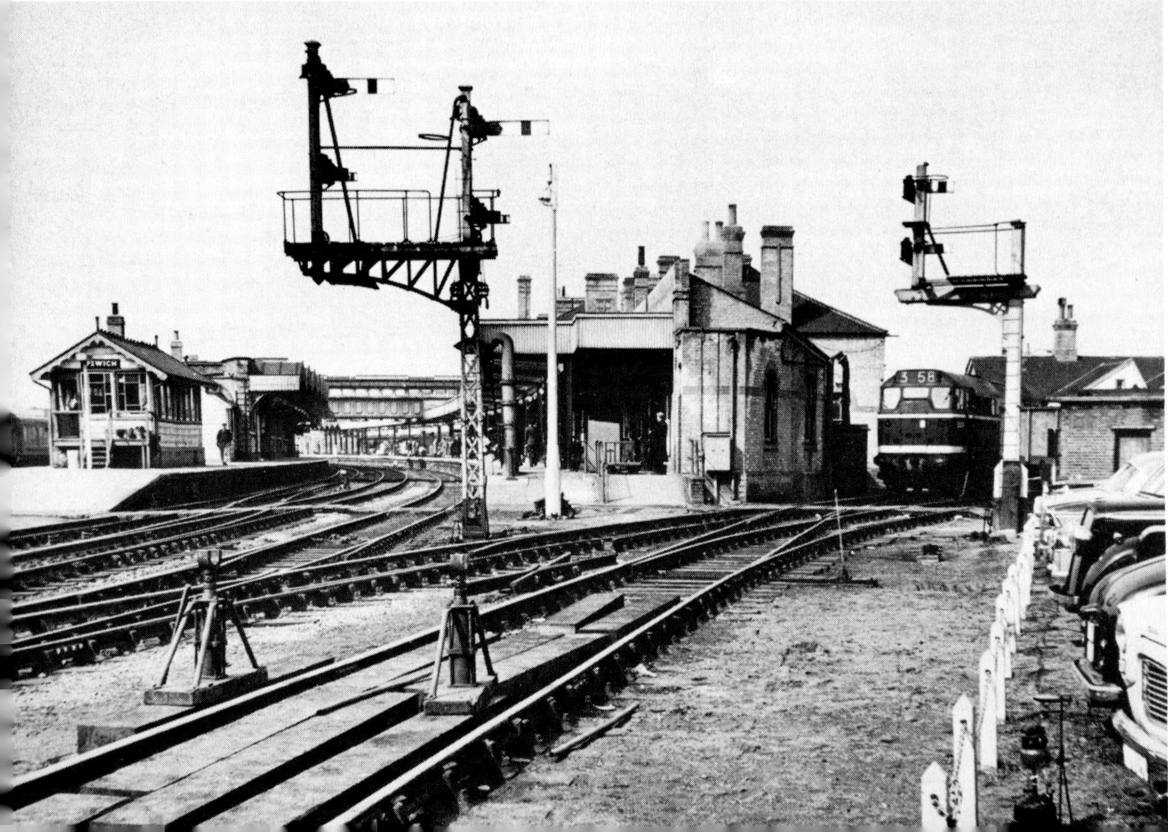

Ipswich is the effective if not the actual junction for the lines to Norwich, Bury St Edmunds, Cambridge, and the East Suffolk main line. These two views were taken from the tunnel mouth, opened on 1 July 1860, the original Ipswich station having been behind the camera at Croft Street. The picture, top left, was taken in 1902; 60 years on, left, the scene had changed but little, most of the buildings being totally unchanged. The T19 has given way in various stages to the Brush diesel and today the scene would be much the same except for the fact that the line in the foreground has been lifted as has the spur on which the Brush diesel is standing.

Above: The Great Eastern Railway's decision to run non-stop trains presented the need for watering facilities: in 1867 water troughs were installed at Halifax Junction.

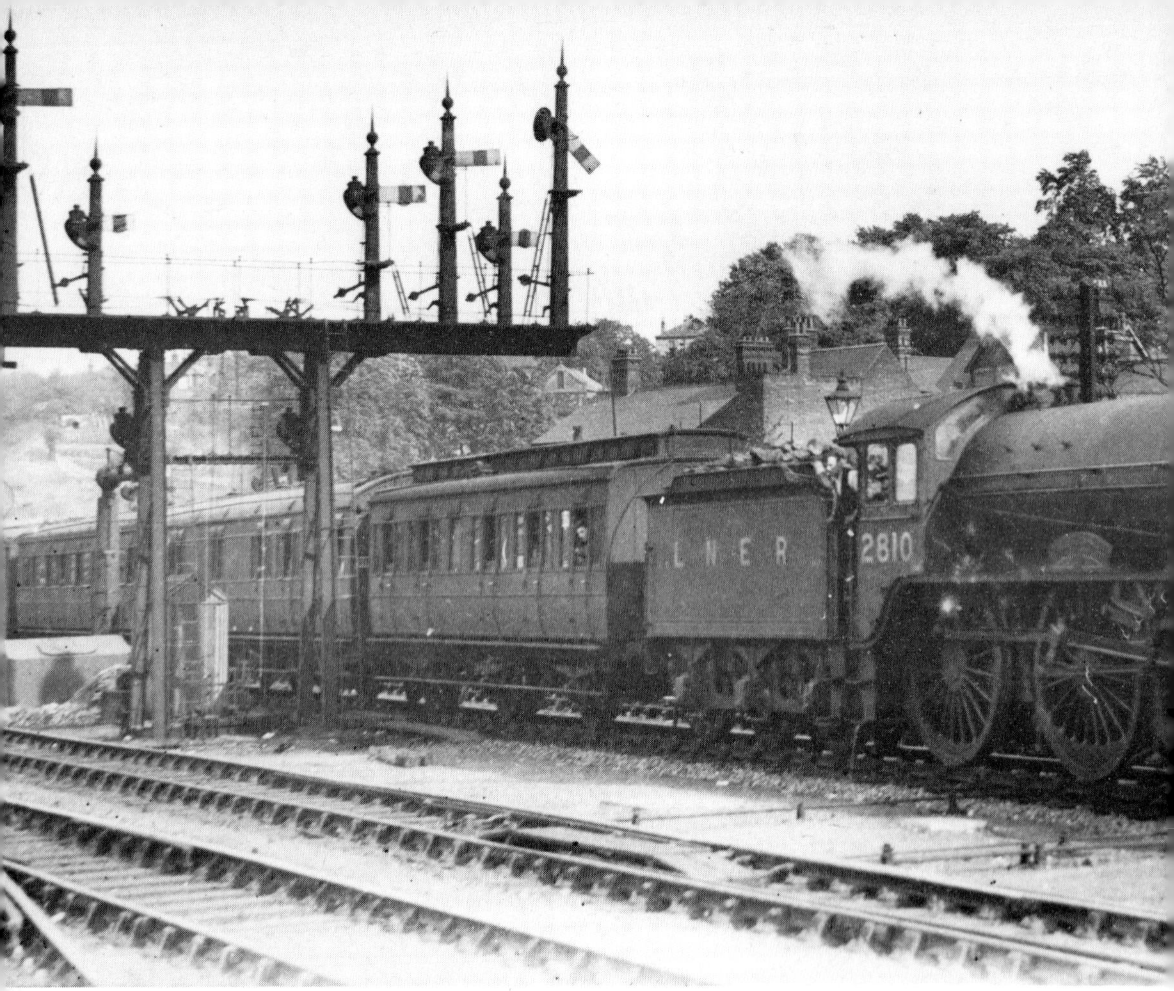
L N E R
2810

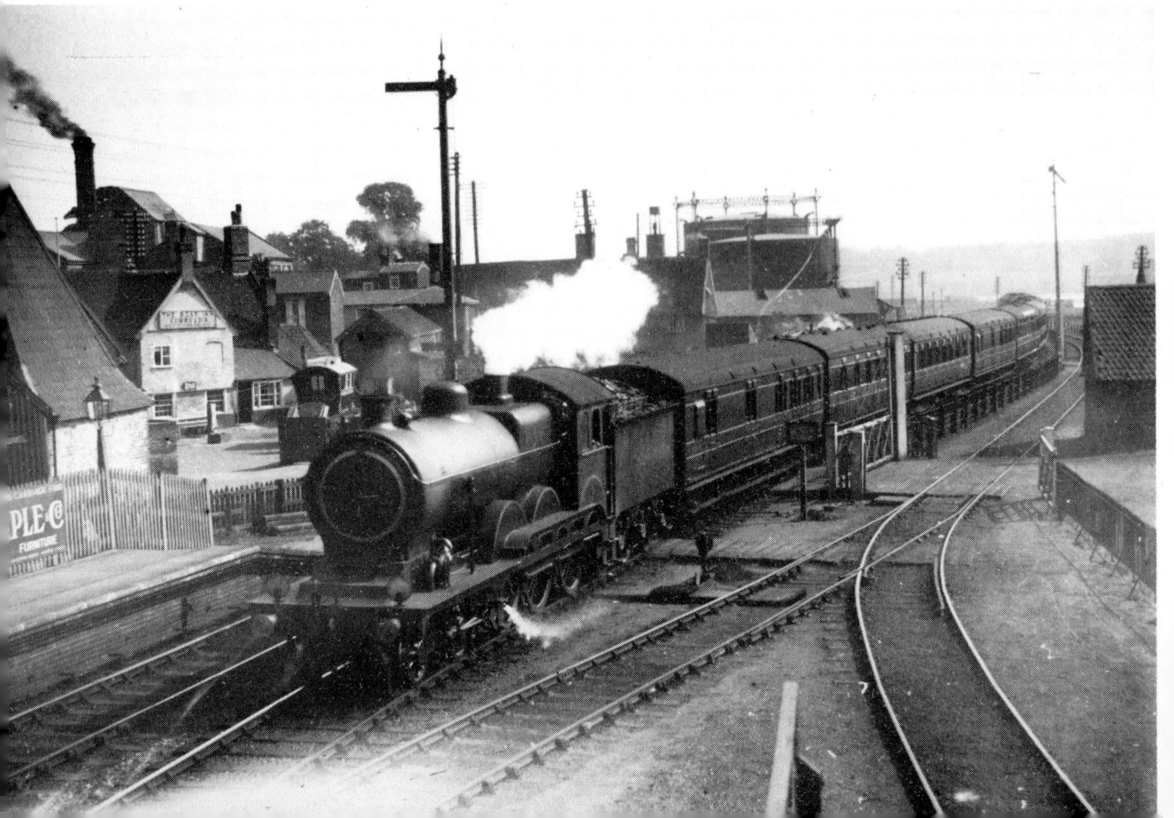
FURNITURE

At Haughley Junction the line to Bury and Cambridge leaves the Norwich line. In the summer of 1931 B17 4-6-0 No 2810 *Honingham Hall* waits at platform 4 with an express for Cambridge. Immediately behind the tender is a somewhat aged six-wheeled clerestory coach – rather surprisingly on an express train, in the 1930s.

Bottom left: Woodbridge is a pleasant country town, famous for its Tide Mill (recently restored), its school and as a yachting centre. In May 1927 Class B12 4-6-0 No 8562 was entering the station from Lowestoft with the 9.40am fast. The building behind the 'Maple' sign is the Woodbridge Cinema, this being the screen end. It seems distinctly possible that the Ealing comedy *The Smallest Show on Earth* was based on this emporium for whenever a northbound train left the station the entire building shook.

Below: This is Ipswich marshalling yard in the early days of nationalisation. Class J39 0-6-0 No 64724 is arriving from Norwich while another J39 waits on the right for its turn to be off. The line in the centre of the picture under the bridge is the East Suffolk main line from which the Felixstowe branch departs at Westerfield. (*East Anglian Daily Times*)

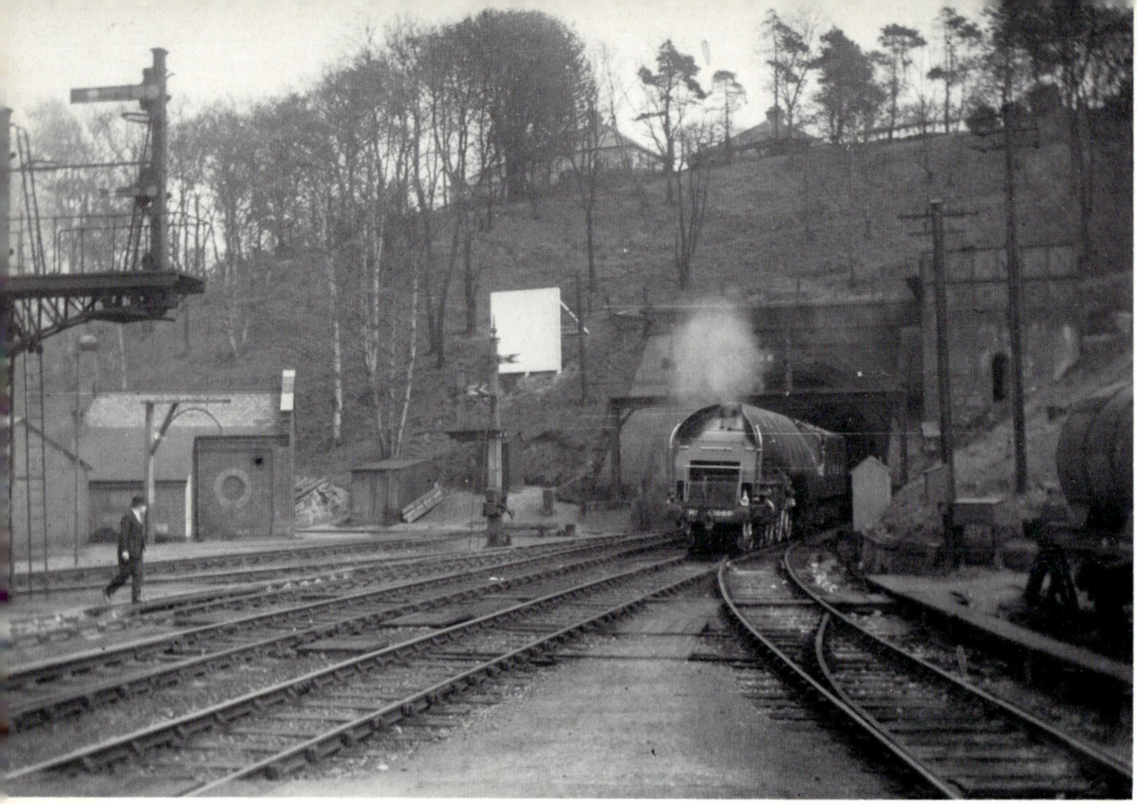

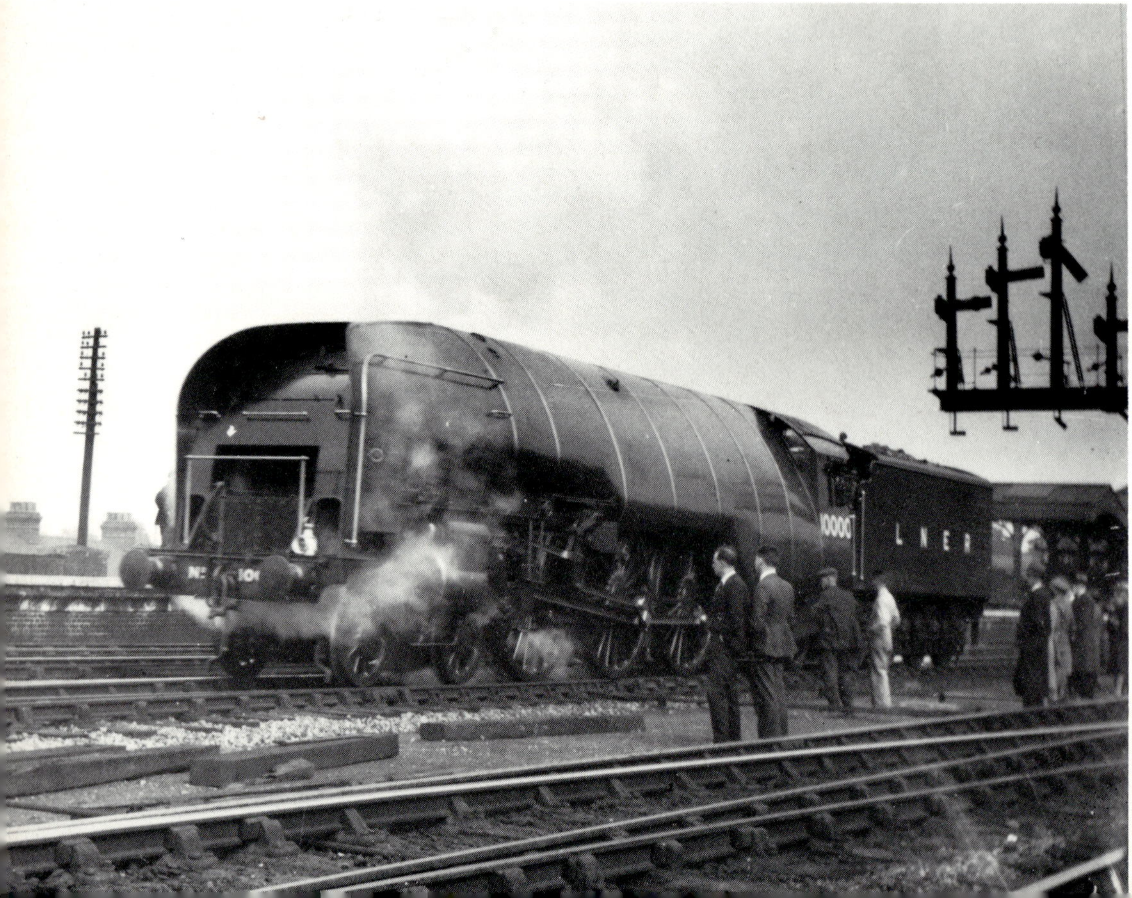
L N E R

The LNER was always very publicity conscious, frequently holding exhibitions at stations on the network, including Ipswich in April 1932; the photograph top left shows the experimental W1 4-6-4 No 10000 bursting from the tunnel and at rest at the end of platform 3. The signal sighting board is still extant: a friend of the author, eager to find an advertising hoarding in the vicinity of the station, thought it would do very nicely! (R. G. Pratt)

Above: A sight which lasted well into nationalisation throughout East Anglia was horse-shunting. The author well remembers this sturdy pair going about their duties until their retirement. (*East Anglian Daily Times*)

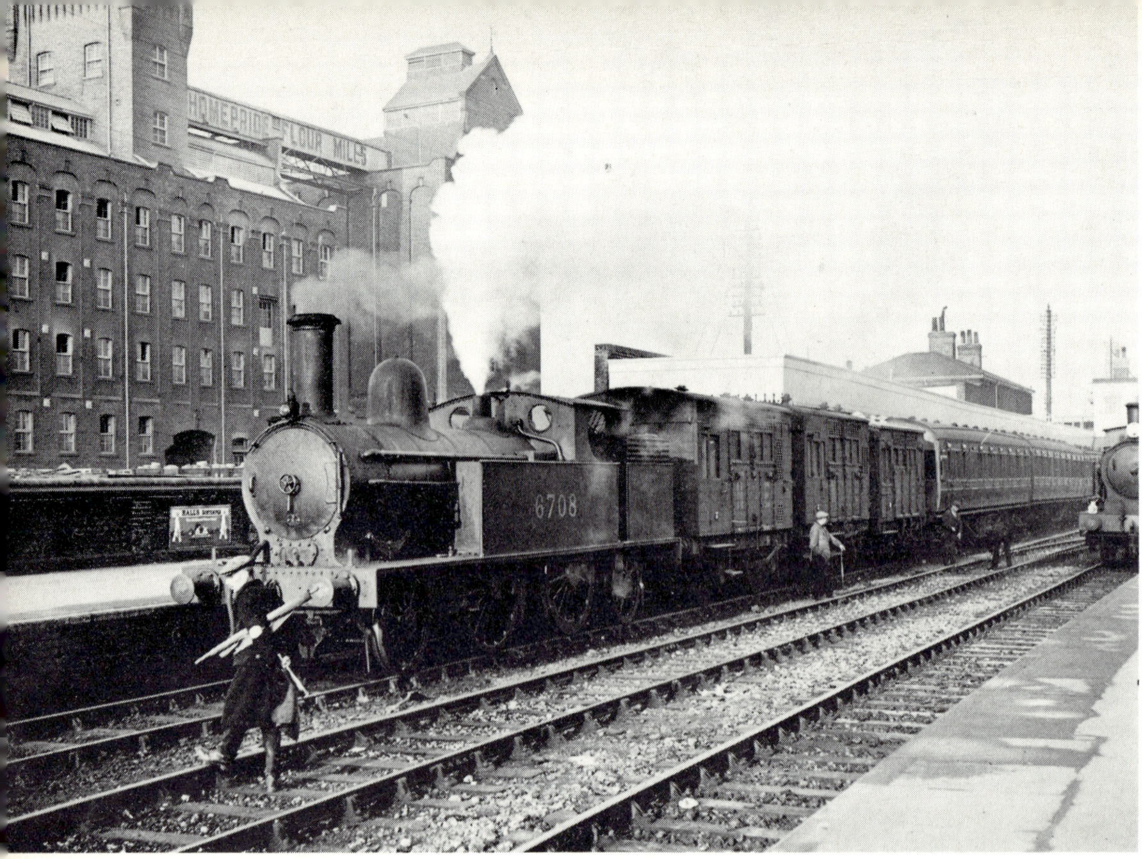
HOMEPRIDE FLOUR MILLS
6708

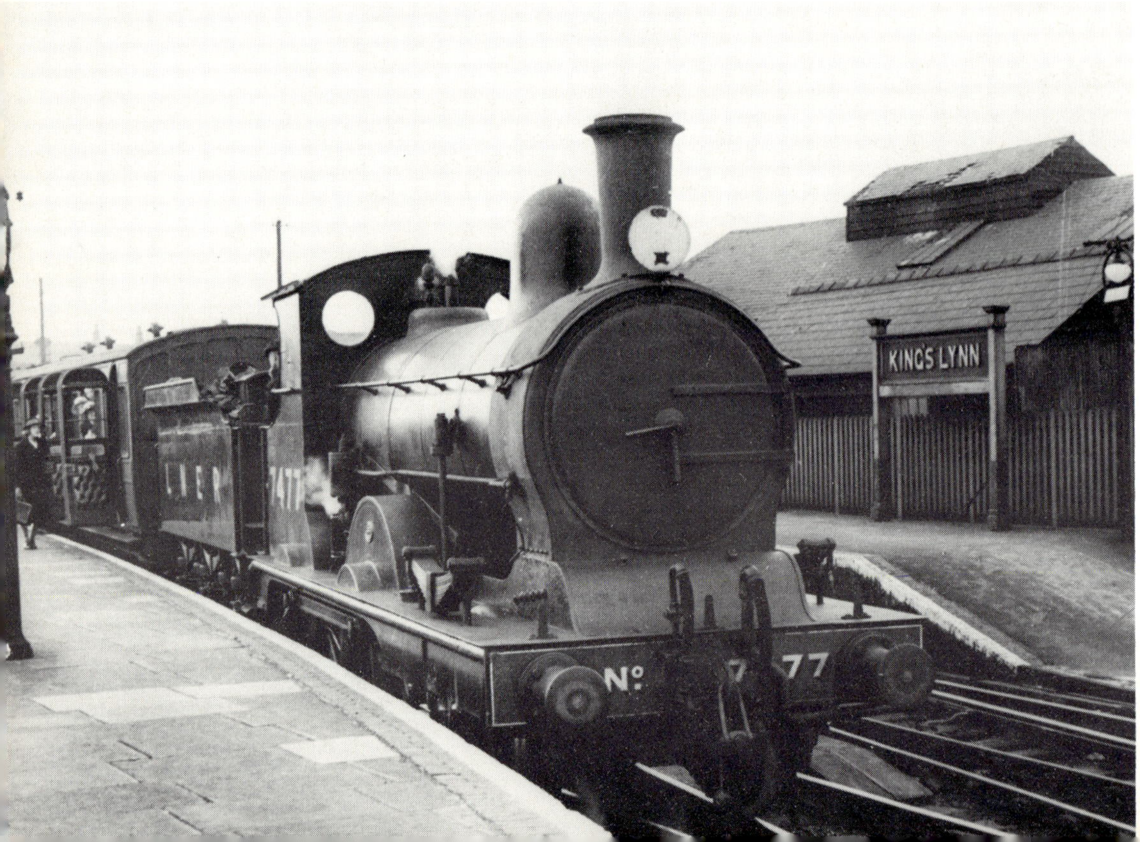
KING'S LYNN
L N E R

Top left: Cambridge on 19 June 1935 with ex-LNWR Class 1P 2–4–2T No 6708 with the 2.07 pm Cambridge to Bletchley train. Cambridge was the deepest the London & North Western penetrated into East Anglia.

Left: From Cambridge through the county and into Norfolk the line runs almost due north to a terminus at Kings Lynn where on 27 March 1937 Class E4 2–4–0 No 7477 is about to depart with a local passenger train. (*H. C. Casserley*)

Above: Hunstanton was the terminus on the North Norfolk coast where in June 1931 the Eastern Belle Pullman train is seen in the station. (*L&GRP*)

South of Wells lay Fakenham which was blessed with two stations, one for the Midland & Great Northern and one for the Great Eastern which is seen on 1 September 1955 with Claud Hamilton 4-4-0 No 62577 awaiting departure with a train for Norwich. (*R. M. Casserley*)

Great Yarmouth had three terminal stations. Beach was the home of the M&GN, South Town was built by the Yarmouth & Haddiscoe Railway and closed in November 1959. Vauxhall was built by the Norfolk & Suffolk Joint Committee and is the only one still in use, where on a damp 14 March 1939 Class D15 4-4-0 No 8884 awaits departure with a stopping passenger train.
(*H. C. Casserley*)

5. CROSS COUNTRY

Saffron Walden had been by-passed by the major railways, the town suffering consequently. The Quaker family of Gibson promoted the Saffron Walden Railway which opened from Audley End to Saffron Walden on 23 November 1865 extending to meet the Great Eastern Railway at Bartlow on 22 October 1866. The junction at Bartlow faced towards Cambridge so the Great Eastern refused to divert freight over the line. The railway went into liquidation in 1869 and was purchased by the Great Eastern on 1 January 1877. In LNER days the line was worked by push-pull units of which one is seen at Saffron Walden station on 7 July 1956. (*H. C. Casserley*)

Class G5 0-4-4T No 67279 rests at Bartlow with a push-pull train on 6 April 1955. The control trailer coach was built by the Great Eastern Railway in May 1897 and converted for the Palace Gates line in March 1924. In July 1958 diesel railbuses took over from the push-pull trains and subsequently worked the line. Passenger services were withdrawn on 7 July 1964 and the line closed completely on 28 December 1964. (*R. M Casserley*)

Saffron Walden on 27 June 1956 where Holden Class G4 0-4-4T No 8105 pauses with a goods train to take water. (*H. C. Casserley*)

At Shelford on the main line from Liverpool Street to Cambridge lay the junction for the cross country Cambridge to Colchester line which opened in various stages between 1849 and 1865 as the Colchester, Stour Valley, Sudbury & Halstead Railway incorporated into the Great Eastern in 1862. On 7 July 1956 J15 0-6-0 No 65390 enters Bartlow with a Cambridge to Colchester train. (*H. C. Casserley*)

Haverhill was the junction between the Great Eastern Railway and the Colne Valley & Halstead Railway where on 15 October 1935 class E4 2–4–0 No 7466 has just received the right away while an unidentified J15 waits for the road. The CV&H cross-country line was closed to goods on 31 October 1966 and to passengers on 6 March 1967. (*H. C. Casserley*)

The Colne Valley & Halstead Railway was opened in two sections from Chappel to Halstead on 16 April 1860 and Halstead to Haverhill on 10 May 1863. It remained totally independent until 1 January 1923 when taken over by the LNER. On 24 May 1956 J15 0–6–0 No 65448 waits at Haverhill with a train for Chappel & Wakes Colne. (*H. C. Casserley*)

The Colchester, Stour Valley, Sudbury & Halstead Railway was responsible for the longest and tallest viaduct in East Anglia at Chappel & Wakes Colne, which is seen here being crossed by a local train, in the charge of a J15. The viaduct has a total of 30 arches of 35ft span and a maximum height of 75ft. It was opened in July 1849. Beyond Sudbury the line is now lifted.

The line from Marks Tey to Sudbury is now worked by dmus, one of which is seen at a forlorn Sudbury in December 1970.

The line from Tivetshall to Beccles opened between 1855 and 1863 as the Waveney Valley Railway and was incorporated into the Great Eastern on 2 March 1863, when the line finally reached Beccles. On 1 September 1951 Class E4 2–4–0 No 62789 leaves Tivetshall with a train from Beccles for Norwich. (*H. C. Casserley*)

The Tivetshall–Beccles line was closed to passengers on 5 January 1953, a wintry day, when Class F3 2–4–2T No. 67128 hauled the last train from Tivetshall to Beccles. (*East Anglian Daily Times*)

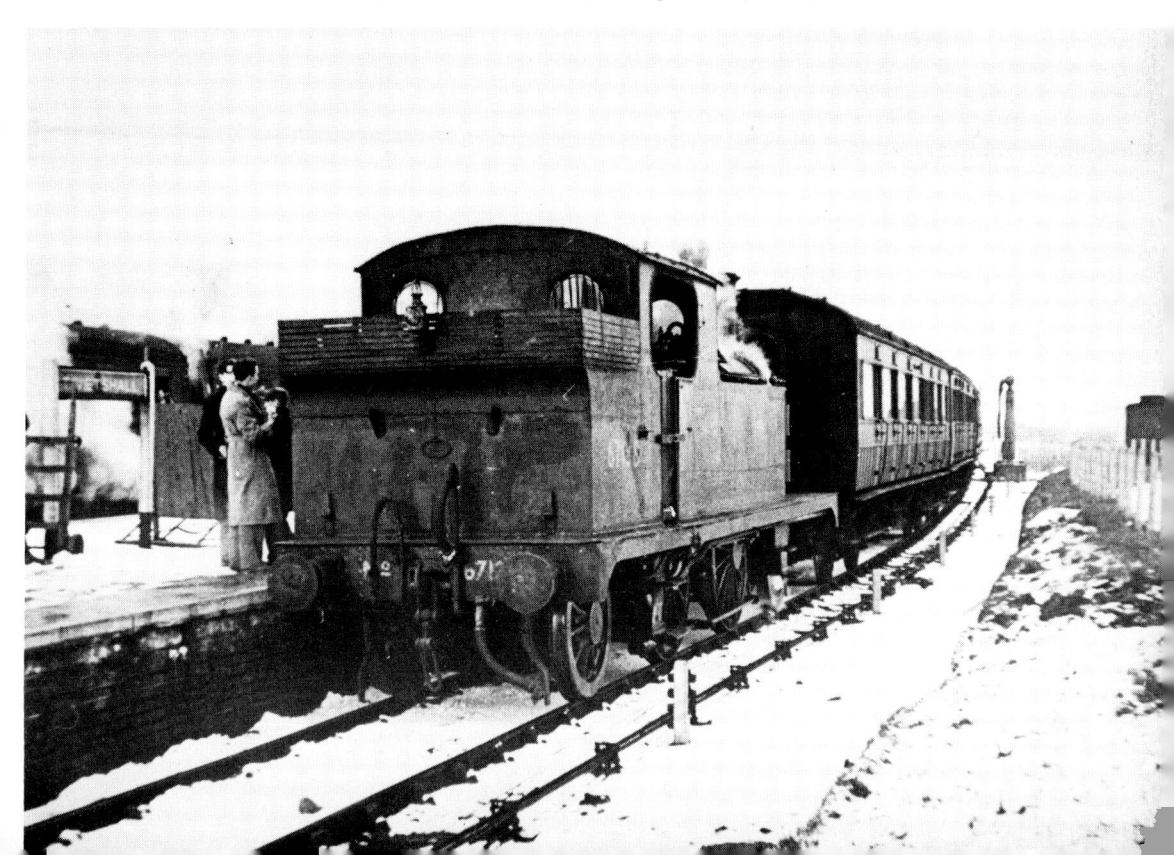

The easternmost point of the Midland & Great Northern was Beach station at Great Yarmouth which is seen in August 1931, looking towards the buffers. (*L&GRP*)

6. THE MIDLAND & GREAT NORTHERN JOINT RAILWAY

On 28 March 1937 Melton Constable-built Class MR 0–6–0T was on shunting duties at the station, still showing its M&GN number plates despite its new ownership. Note the somersault signal of Great Northern design. The station is now razed, the site being used as a car park and bus station. (*H. C. Casserley*)

Shortly after leaving Beach station trains for Lowestoft traversed the five-span 800ft-long viaduct over Breydon Water. When this viaduct fell due for renovation in 1956 the line was severed so that M&GN line trains could no longer serve the Norfolk & Suffolk joint line to Lowestoft. (L&GRP)

Cromer Beach station was the most northerly on the M&GN. At around the turn of the century an express is about to leave in the charge of No 26, a 4-4-0 built to the design of the Lynn & Fakenham Railway by Beyer Peacock and Co Ltd.

In the mid 1940s Class B 4–4–0T No 20 was awaiting departure from Cromer Beach station. Originally delivered to the Lynn & Fakenham Railway on 3 October 1881 it was named *King's Lynn* and cost the princely sum of £811 12s 1d. (*H. C. Casserley*)

Melton Constable (the 'Crewe of East Anglia') with Great Central Railway Class 11 4–4–0 No 6041 with an express from Great Yarmouth to the Midlands on 13 March 1939. Under LNER ownership these locomotives became Class D9. (*H. C. Casserley*)

These two photographs were taken from practically the same spot but two years apart. In the upper one Class 4 0–6–0 No 71 passes Melton Constable West box with a freight train from Spalding in May 1937, while in the lower one a Midland Railway Class C 4–4–0 arrives from Cromer Beach with a passenger train on 13 March 1939. When the LNER took over the line the M&GN locomotive stock had their numbers prefixed by 0, hence this locomotive became No 042. (*L&GRP; H. C. Casserley*)

This graceful 4-4-0 with 6ft driving wheels owes its origins to the Lynn & Fakenham Railway for whom the original batch of Class A engines were built by Beyer Peacock in 1883 at a cost of £3000 each. All were delivered in March 1882 finished in the company's passenger livery of pale green. Four more were delivered to the Lynn & Fakenham's successor the Eastern & Midlands in 1883. Interestingly the first two batches were not equipped with front couplings for hauling tender first. No 34 was built for the Eastern & Midlands in June 1886 finished in that company's livery of brown, lined with black and chrome yellow, in which condition it is seen at Cromer. (*L&GRP*)

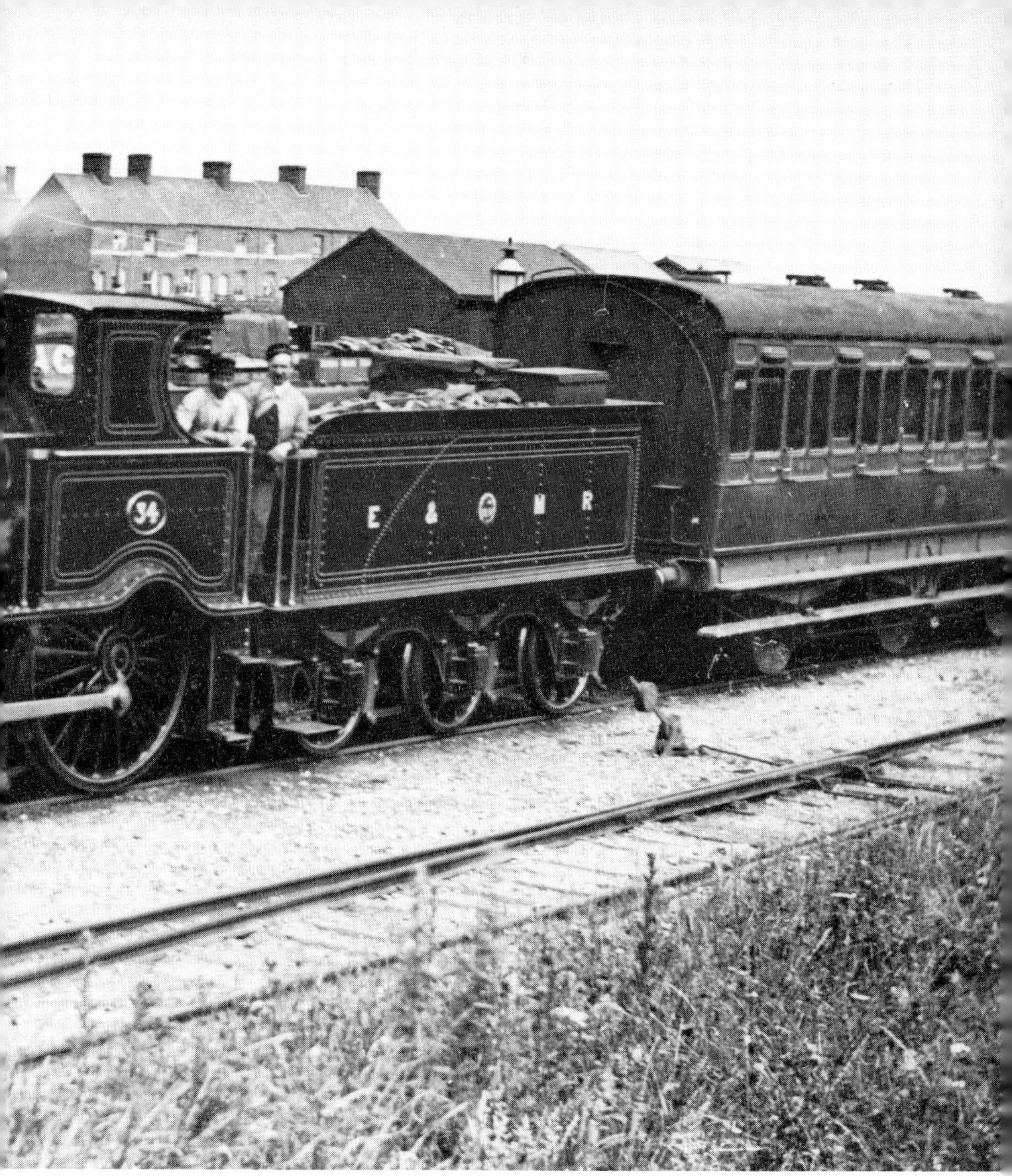
34
E & M R

The line from Peterborough joined the main M&GN system at Sutton Bridge where on 27 March 1937 Ivatt Great Northern Class J4 0–6–0 No 4154 blows off impatiently. (*H. C. Casserley*)

The M&GN system linked with the Great Northern line at Spalding and there on 16 September 1933 ex-Great Central Railway Robinson Class B5 4–6–0 No 5187 and Ivatt Class C1 Atlantic No 4407 stand on parallel tracks. (*H. C. Casserley*)

On its constitution the M&GN inherited a motley selection of locomotives from its constituent companies. The Class B 4-4-0Ts were delivered to the Yarmouth & Norfolk Railway and Lynn & Fakenham Railway by the makers Hudswell Clark, and Rogers between 1878 and 1881. No two were identical; the one portrayed owed its original parentage to the Yarmouth & Norfolk in 1879 by whom it was named *Martham*. (*L&GRP*)

Five of the Class A engines were rebuilt from 1893 with Class C boilers, being known as Class A Rebuilt. Of these No 28 is seen on the coaling point at South Lynn shed in May 1927. In all, the M&GN had 182 miles 32 chains of route, of which no less than 109 miles 18 chains were of single track! Not surprisingly this was the cause of serious operating difficulties which were partly offset by the fitting of Whittaker automatic tablet exchange equipment which is seen on the tender of No 28. (*L&GRP*)

Above: In 1894 Sharp Stewart supplied 26 Midland Railway Class 2203 6ft 6in 4-4-0s to the Midland & Great Northern where they became Class C; No 5 is seen near Cromer in 1923 with a local passenger train. (*L&GRP*)

Top right: From 1910 some of the Class C 4-4-0s were rebuilt with G6 boilers and new cabs; in this guise No 38 is leaving South Lynn with a Yarmouth train in May 1937 wearing the umber livery introduced in 1930. (*L&GRP*)

Right: M&GN Class D were 5ft 2in 0-6-0s which came in two batches from Neilson & Co (Nos 58-65) in 1896 and Kitson & Co (66-73) in 1898, originally being a Midland Railway Johnson Class 2284 design. In May 1937 No 61 in its original form approaches Melton Constable with a freight train. (*L&GRP*)

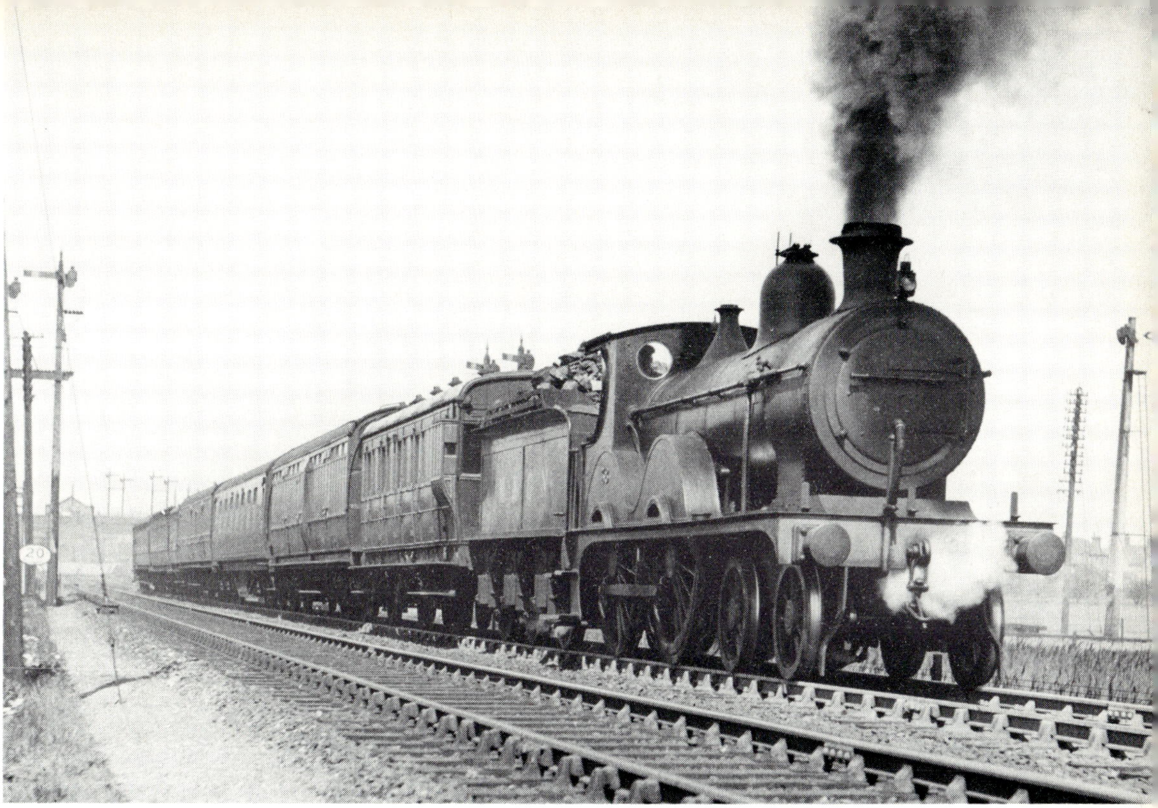
20

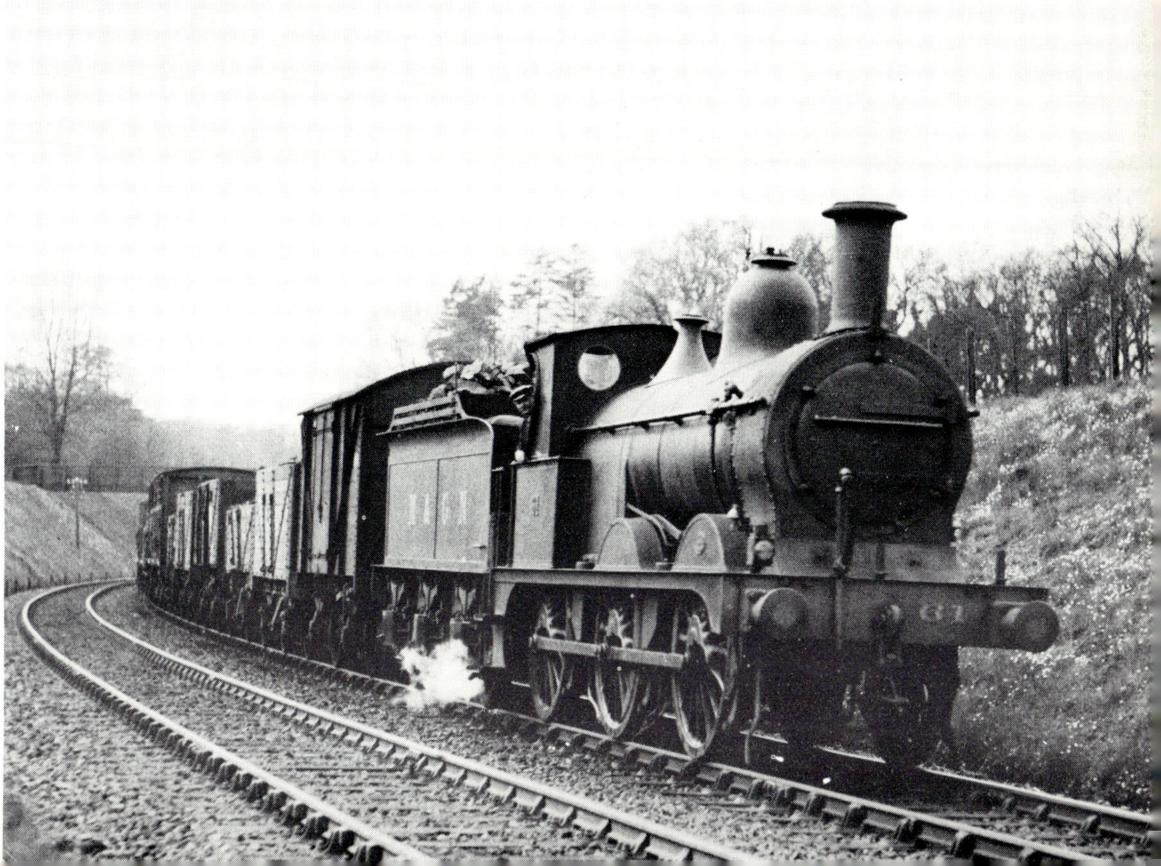

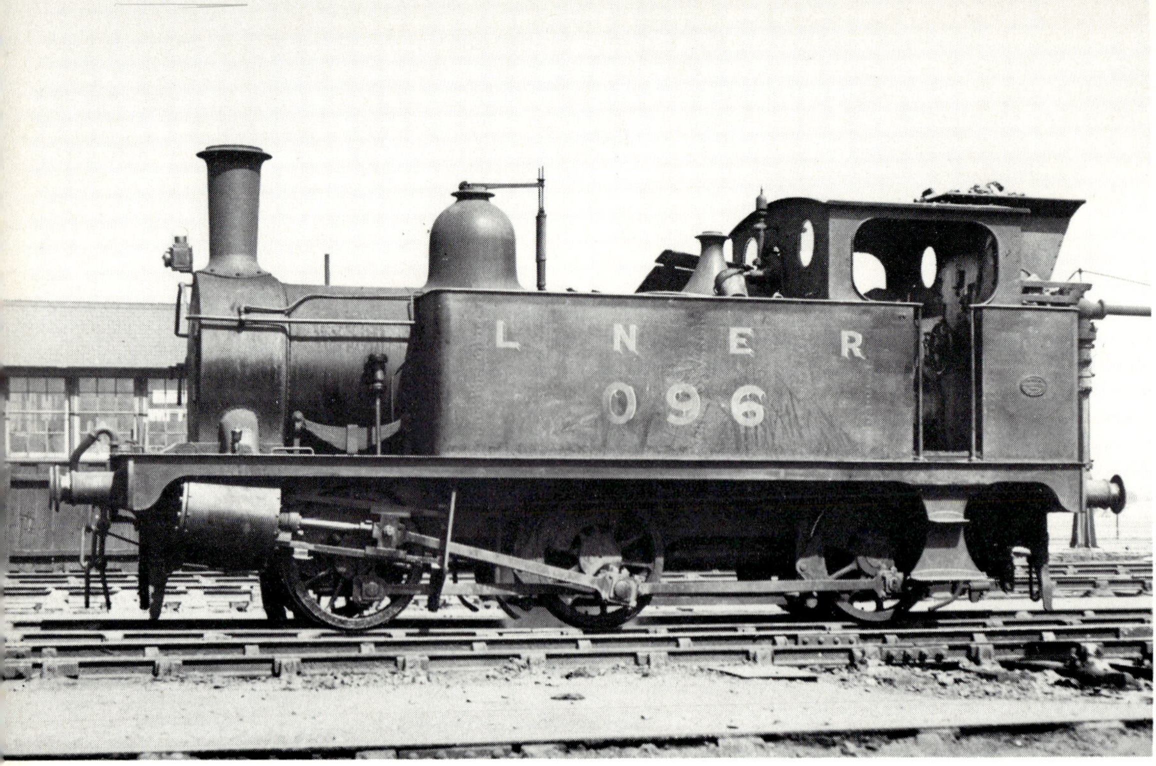
L N E R
096

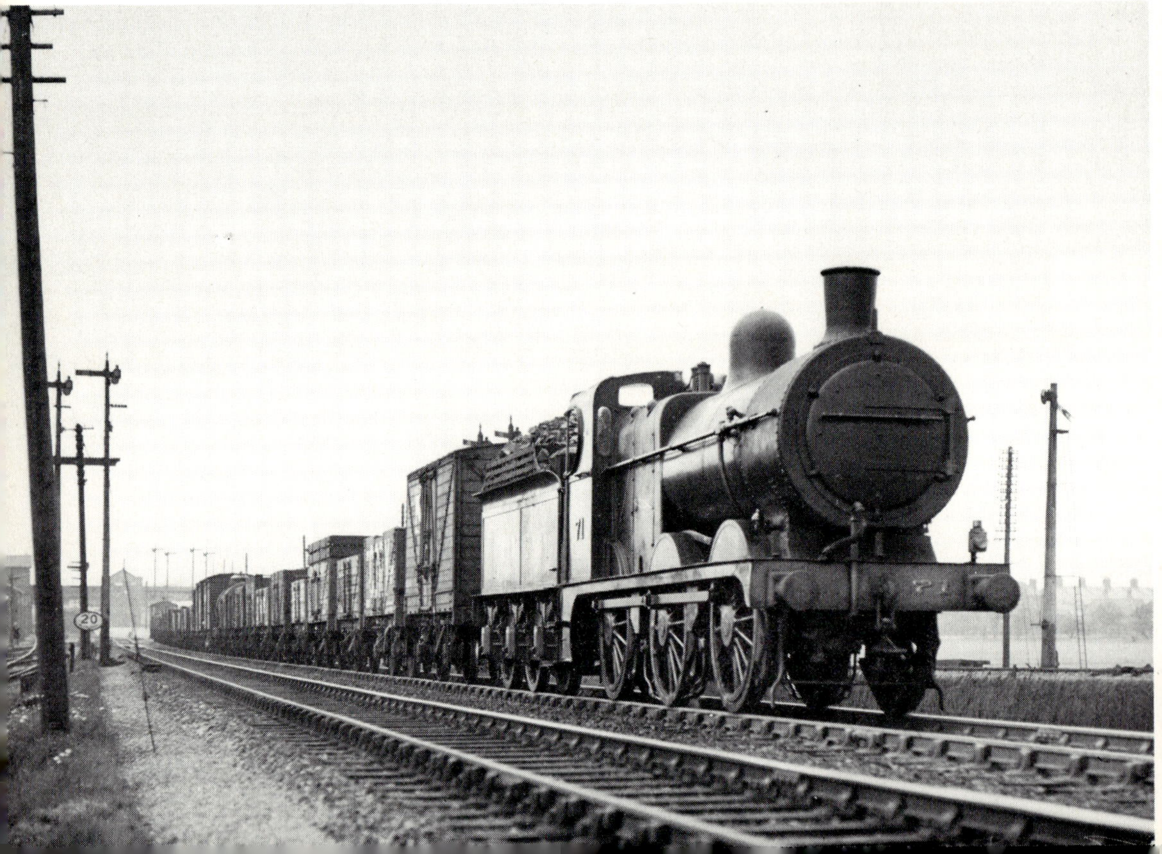
20

Top left: In October 1897 the first of the Class MR 0–6–0Ts, which eventually totalled 19 engines, appeared from Melton Constable, officially a rebuild but, for all practical purposes, a new locomotive, being numbered 14A. Built to carry 800 gallons of water and 1½ tons of coal, some were fitted with hopper bunkers when they could carry two tons of coal, as No 096. Under the LNER they became Class J93 and three passed to BR. (*L&GRP*)

Left: In May 1937 No 71, as rebuilt with higher pressure boiler and with stovepipe chimney and extended smokebox, is leaving South Lynn. This locomotive and No 69 became LNER Class J41. (*L&GRP*)

Above: In 1900 Dübs & Co built 12 5ft 2in GNR Ivatt 0–6–0s for the M&GN which classified them Class DA. They were the only M&GN locomotives to have both the engine and tender fitted with the automatic vacuum brake. Under the LNER they became Class J3. In May 1937 No 084 is seen leaving Spalding with a passenger train for Kings Lynn. (*L&GRP*)

London, Tilbury & Southend train hauled by 4–4–2T No 40 *Blackhorse Road*, built in 1897 by Sharp Stewart, near Chalkwell with an up train bound for Fenchurch Street. By 1896 all coaches were electrically lit, one of only two steam lines so equipped at that time, since most railways had adopted gas lighting to replace oil lamps, before converting to electricity. (*L&GRP*)

Under LMS ownership No 42 *Commercial Road* had become No 2151 and is seen at Shoeburyness. At this time it was still customary for the locomotive to carry a destination board.

7. THE LONDON, TILBURY & SOUTHEND RAILWAY

The first LTSR bogie coaches were introduced in 1903 but Midland stock was used on trains from St Pancras. MR clerestory stock is seen behind LTSR 4-4-2T No 37 *Woodgrange* in 1910. London Tilbury & Southend locomotive livery was light green with purple brown borders round the tanks; the boiler bands were also purple brown as were the wheel centres which were edged in red. No 80 *Thundersley* built by Robert Stephenson in 1909 is preserved at Bressingham Steam Museum as part of the National Collection. (*L&GRP*)

Under the LMS, freight and some parcels workings on the LTS line were in the hands of Fowler 0–6–0s, this policy continuing in BR days. On 29 August 1959 No 44270 is seen at Purfleet with a down parcels train.
(*G. M. Kichenside*)

On 28 June 1958 an unidentified Fairburn 2–6–4T passes Tilbury East Junction with a Fenchurch Street–Southend train. (*G. M. Kichenside*)

The essentially suburban character of much of the line can be seen in this view of Stanier 4MT 2–6–4T No 42509 at Bromley-by-Bow with the 11.55am from Fenchurch Street to Thorpe Bay on 8 September 1956. The destination boards had now disappeared.
(*G. M. Kichenside*)

From Manningtree to Parkeston Quay and Harwich ran the Great Eastern's outlet to the Continent. In August 1934 Class B17 4-6-0 No 2822 *Alnwick Castle* leaves Dovercourt with the Harwich to York boat train.

8. SEAPORT BRANCHES

Manningtree station on 24 March 1951 as B1 4-6-0 No 61363 takes the Harwich branch with the down Day Continental. (*H. N. James*)

The original plans for a railway to Felixstowe were promoted as an independent line. However it was eventually opened as a branch of the Great Eastern Railway; passenger services commenced on 1 May 1877, two months before the contract deadline. The line is seen here, above, under construction. (*G. Cordy*)

It was operated by three diminutive 2–4–0 side tank locomotives built by the Yorkshire Engine Co, No 1 *Tomline*, No 2 *Orwell* and No 3 *Felixstowe*. Illustrated below is No 2. All three passed to Great Eastern ownership and numbered 808 to 810. (*L&GRP*)

At Parkeston Quay in September 1938 is the LNER steamer *Malines*, later torpedoed off Port Said in 1942.

In LNER days J15 0-6-0s took over Felixstowe line passenger traffic and No 7641 is seen leaving Felixstowe Beach with a rake of six-wheel carriages in August 1931.

In August 1912 the Great Eastern applied to Parliament for powers to double the Felixstowe branch throughout from Westerfield to Felixstowe Town. Apart from Spring Road viaduct in Ipswich, which had been the only major engineering feat in the construction of the branch, there would have been few problems, but the outbreak of war in 1914 prevented the Great Eastern from proceeding with its plans. The three-arch viaduct was 60ft high at the parapet and consumed 800,000 bricks in its making. In this view Class L1 2–6–4T No 67708 is crossing with a train from Felixstowe to Ipswich around 1950. At that time the town was still blessed with trolleybuses and there was a remarkable lack of road traffic. (*East Anglian Daily Times*)

9. TITLED TRAINS

Overleaf: In the early 1930s Class B17 4–6–0 No 2824 *Lumley Castle* heads the Flushing Continental through the Essex countryside on its way to Parkeston Quay. Note the early style of headboard and the two Pullman cars in the middle of the train.

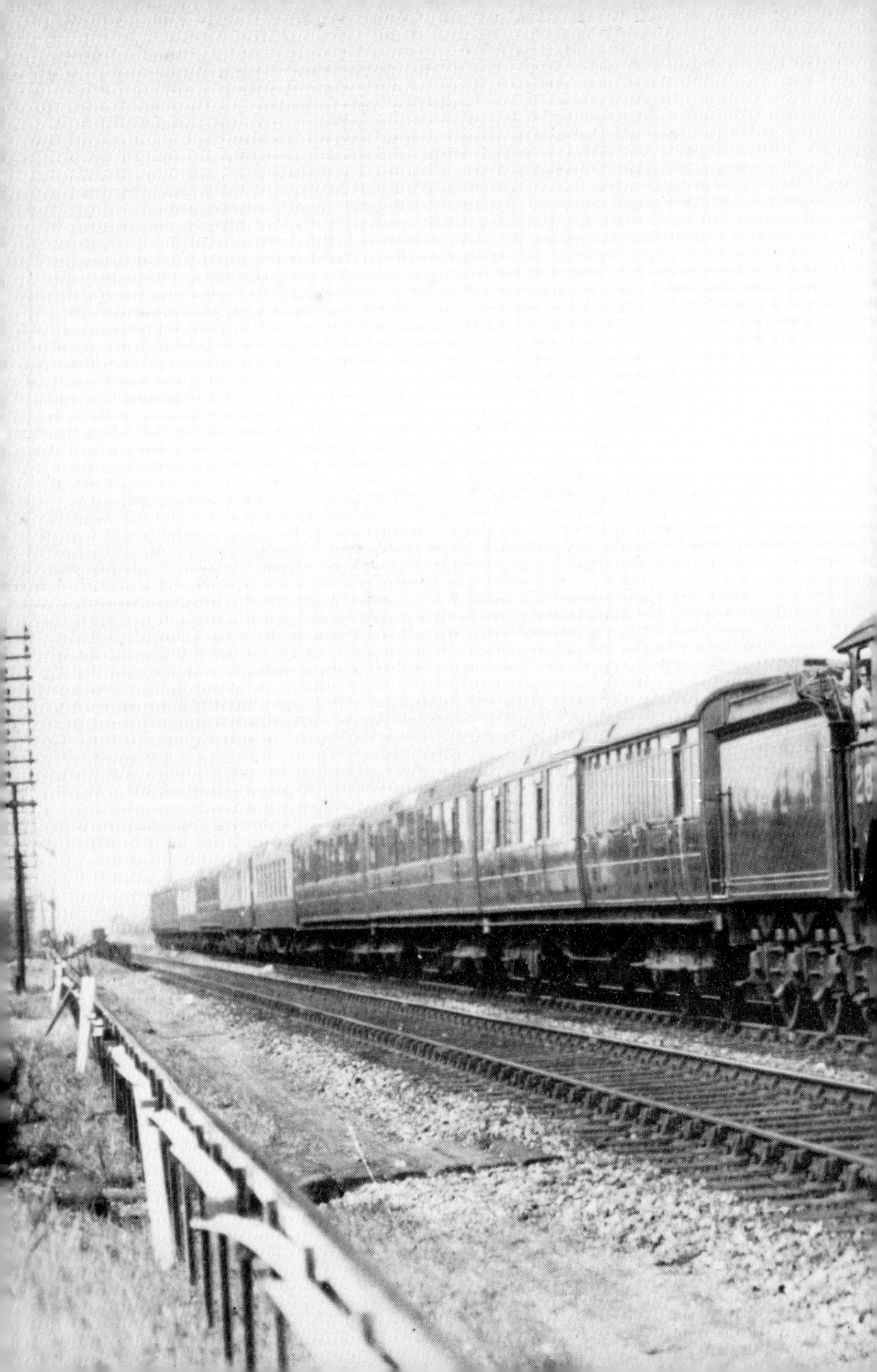

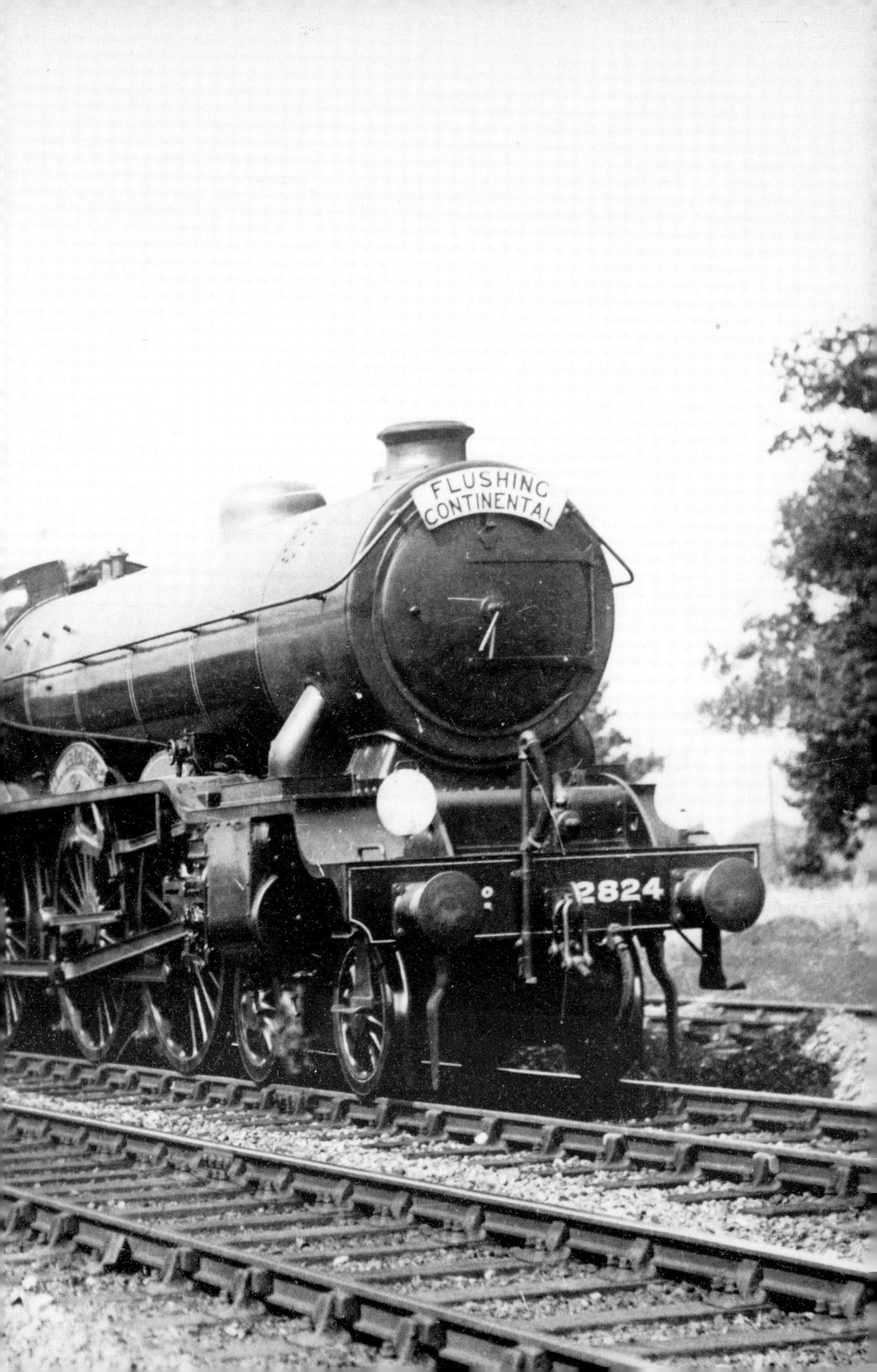
FLUSHING
CONTINENTAL
2824

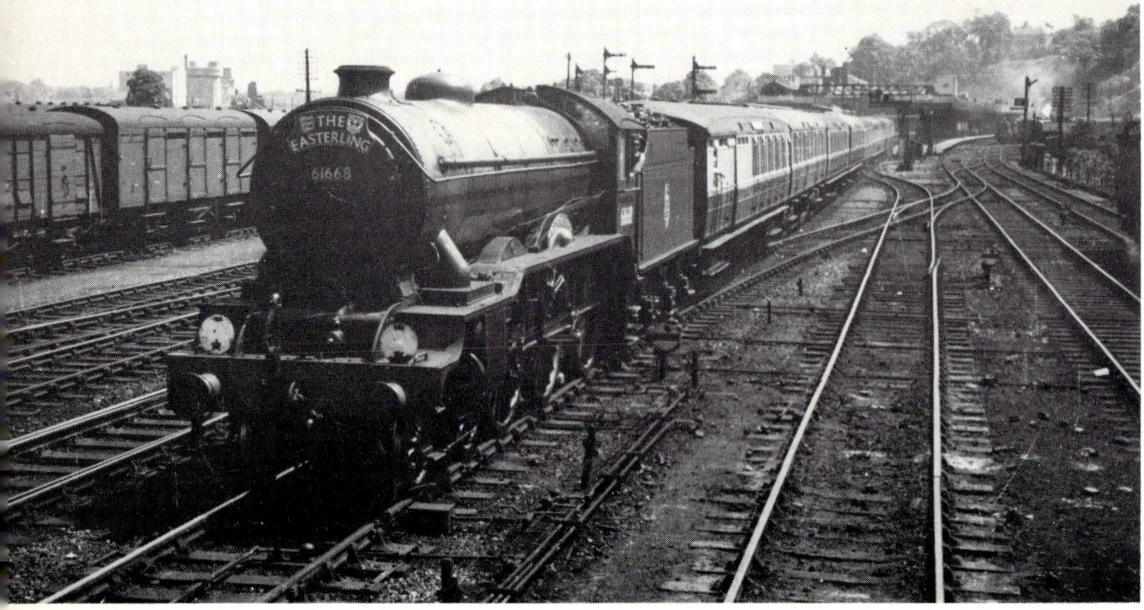
THE EASTERLING
61668

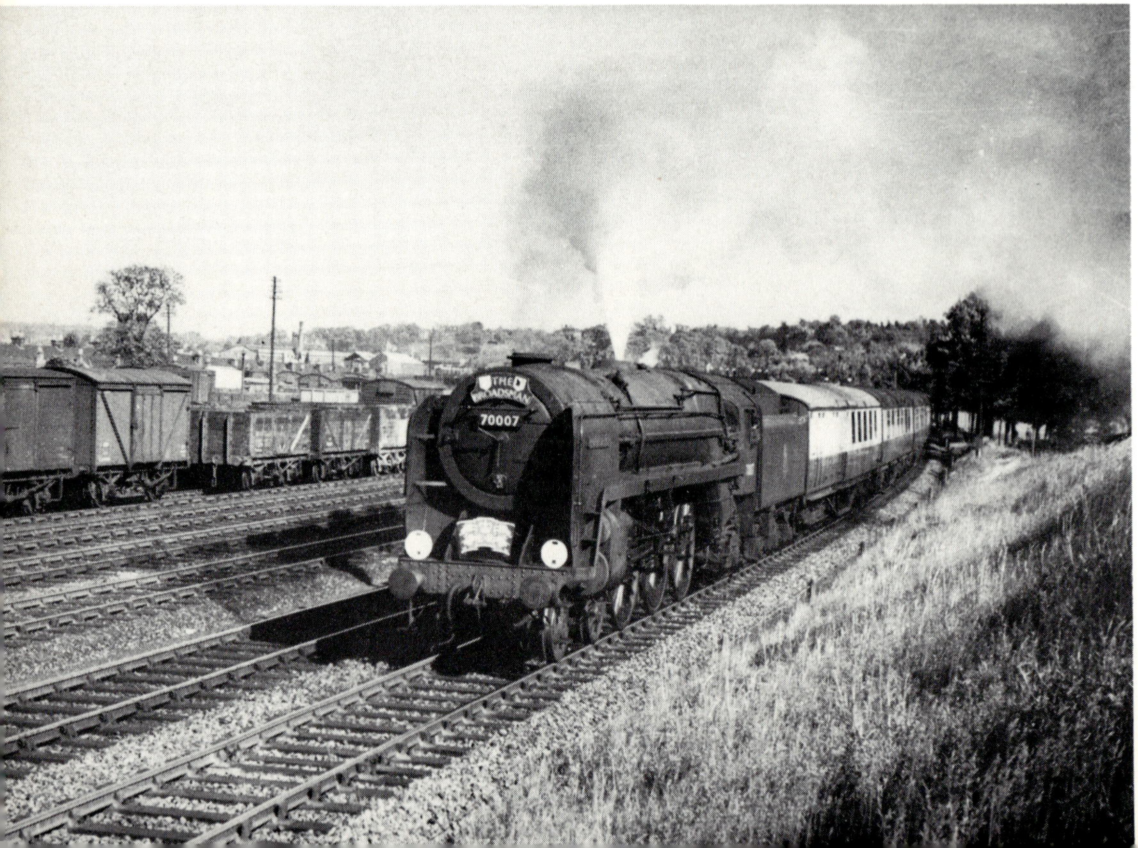
THE
70007

Top left: 1 July 1952 and Class B17/4 No 61668 *Bradford City* passes Ipswich station with the down Easterling, the only express not to stop at Ipswich. (*H. N. James*)

Above: Parkeston Quay in 1951. The first British Railways standard locomotive No 70000 *Britannia* is about to leave with the up Hook Continental. (*East Anglian Daily Times*)

Left: On 28 May 1953 No 70007 *Coeur de Lion* passes Ipswich yard with the down Broadsman. This was Coronation year, and the locomotive is carrying an additional decorative headboard. The train is composed of Gresley teak coaches repainted in the original BR express coach livery of crimson and cream, irreverently known as 'blood & custard' or 'egg and tomato'! (*H. N. James*)

10. BYWAYS

The Maldon, Witham & Braintree Railway opened for goods on 15 August 1848 and passengers on 2 October 1848, the Eastern Counties Railway judiciously allowing the newcomer to cross its lines on the level at Witham, effectively creating two branch lines as through traffic required reversal at Witham. Yet it then made no effort to promote the Maldon end of the line as had been promised to the promoters. The photograph depicts the essentially rural character of the line which shows Class N2 0–6–2T No 69624 leaving Witham for Braintree & Bocking on 26 May 1956.

Dr Beeching planned to axe the line but vigorous local activity opposed it and the line survived to be electrified in 1980 and is now served by emus direct to Liverpool Street which have taken over from the dmu service operated from 1958. For the moment the future seems secure. (*H. C. Casserley*)

A short distance down the main line from Witham lies Kelvedon, the railhead of the Kelvedon, Tiptree & Tollesbury Light Railway which opened to Tollesbury on 8 October 1904, and to the pier on 15 May 1907. This view shows Tollesbury station looking towards the pier in May 1935. The spartan platform accommodation was typical of the line (Inworth had a bare platform!) Decline began in the early 1920s when a bus service provided more than equal competition for the railway when trains ran slowly, and made frequent stops for shunting and opening gates; antique centre gangway coaches and conductor guards did little to promote a good image. (L&GRP)

In 1928 improved stock was acquired from the Wisbech & Upwell Tramway, an example of which is seen here at Kelvedon low level on 19 August 1958; passenger traffic continued to decline and services ceased on 7 May 1953. Freight was finally withdrawn on 1 October 1962, and the line was lifted. (L&GRP)

Fordham, on the cross country line between Ely and Bury St Edmunds, was a double junction, one line forming the link from Barnwell Junction while the other was the branch to Mildenhall. On 22 September 1956 Class E4 2–4–0 No 62796 is seen above at Mildenhall and below upon arrival back at Fordham. Diesel multiple-units took over the service in 1958, later superseded by Maybach-engined railbuses until the line fell victim to the Beeching axe and closed to passengers on 18 June 1962.
(H. C. Casserley)

To the north of Cambridgeshire lay the Wisbech & Upwell Tramway which was unique in Britain. The motive power was what appeared to be a smoking guards van. The law required that all working parts of the locomotive on an open unfenced railway should be concealed for safety. The result was the tram locomotive, two classes of which operated on the line. The photograph shows Class Y6 0–4–0T No 7132 passing through Outwell on 27 June 1929. Designed by Worsdell the locomotives were built between 1883–1897 as Great Eastern Railway Class G15 becoming Y6 under LNER ownership. Two passed to British Railways. The line opened to Outwell on 20 June 1883 continuing to Upwell on 3 September 1884. Further extensions were planned but were never built.
(H. C. Casserley)

By 1903 loads had increased necessitating the introduction of 0–6–0 tram locomotives (later LNER Class J70) designed by James Holden. On 25 August 1950 No 68217 is seen at Wisbech. The line had a 12mph speed restriction and to ensure this limit the locomotives were fitted with governors which cut off steam when speed reached 12mph. Passenger services ceased on 31 December 1927. Apart from an experiment with a double-ended sentinel railcar in 1930 the tram engines retained their monopoly of the line until 1952, when a Drewry diesel shunter with skirts and cowcatchers appeared, followed by another after a year of trials. Closure finally came on 23 May 1966. (H. C. Casserley)

Four-wheeled carriages were used on the Wisbech & Upwell Tramway in the first year but a pair of bogie coaches was introduced a year later. They eventually went to the Kelvedon & Tollesbury Railway. One, seen here, survived for preservation and was used in the film *The Titfield Thunderbolt* but was later broken up. (*L&GRP*)

It was said that the Mid Suffolk Light Railway started from nowhere and ended in the middle of a field. The jibe was not all together unjustified for Haughley is but a large village, the station being about 1½ miles away. The author remembers changing trains there one Christmas at the age of six or seven only to see the connection departing. As there was a two hour wait, a walk into the village resulted in finding precisely nothing! The line petered out in a field beyond Laxfield. The first train ran on 29 January 1908 and the line had three 0–6–0Ts, Nos 1–3, built by Hudswell Clarke to a fairly standard design. They were painted deep red, lined out in yellow and vermilion with black edging and gilt lettering. On 28 July 1915 No 2 is seen leaving Haughley for Laxfield with the 5.52 pm train. It is probable that military goods were being conveyed as an army corporal seems to be supervising the movement.

Class J17 0–6–0 No 65447 at Laxfield on 1 September 1951 with a passenger train. Note the six-wheel coaches. To this locomotive fell the duty of hauling the last train when the end came on 27 July 1952. (*H. C. Casserley*)

For all its shortcomings the Mid Suffolk line had charm as can be seen in this photograph of Stonham Aspall station on 1 September 1951. (*H. C. Casserley*)

The 5½ mile Framlingham branch from Campsea Ash near Wickham Market on the East Suffolk main line was opened on 1 June 1859. The terminus at Framlingham was inconveniently placed and the line was thus easy prey to road competition. Passenger facilities ceased on 30 November 1952 some seven months after this photograph taken at Campsea Ash which shows an F6 2–4–2T shunting the branch train. The goods shed is now a car body repair shop. There was one moment of glory for the line in May 1956 when the royal train spent the night at Marlesford during a tour of East Anglia by the Duke of Edinburgh. A daily freight survived to all stations on the branch with the exception of Parham until 19 April 1956 when all services finally ceased and the track was then lifted. (H. W. Moffat)

SOUTHWOLD RAILWAY TRAIN.
SEP 1879 - APRIL 1929.

Left: When the East Suffolk Railway refused to build a branch from Halesworth to Southwold local landowners and businessmen decided to promote a tramway which became the only narrow gauge railway in East Anglia. The Southwold Railway was opened on 24 September 1879 and closed little more than 50 years later after a chequered career. Built to a gauge of 3ft the word eccentric serves well to describe this $8\frac{3}{4}$ mile line which appears to have run with but a scant observance of a timetable. Throughout its life the railway had but four locomotives, three built by Sharp Stewart and one by Manning Wardle. Typical of the eccentricity of the Southwold is that Nos 2 and 3, respectively *Halesworth* and *Blyth* entered service in 1879 (both 2–4–0 tanks) followed by No 1 *Southwold* a 2–4–2 tank in 1893. The last locomotive came from Manning Wardle in 1919, No 4 *Wenhaston* an 0–6–2 tank. Originally finished in green the locomotives were later painted in Great Eastern Railway colours and finally black, with the exception of No 4 which was dark green. This photograph shows No 1 at Wenhaston station with a typical mixed train of goods wagons and tramway style balcony end coaches. A major downfall of the line was its speed restriction of 16mph, which took its toll from 1926 when bus services operated over the same route and were allowed to travel at 20mph, and offered more convenient services. In some respects the railway was its own worst enemy, refusing to build a harbour branch at Southwold until 1914. Twice offers of purchase were refused, in 1893 by the Great Eastern Railway and in 1923 by the LNER. But in 1929 the latter company refused to buy the line and it closed on 12 April. Various attempts at resuscitation were made to no avail and virtually everything went for war salvage in 1941/42.

Above: The Aldeburgh branch was $8\frac{1}{2}$ miles in length from Saxmundham on the East Suffolk main line. The child of the East Suffolk Railway it was initially intended to serve only Leiston, four miles distant, opening on 1 June 1859, but in the same year authority was obtained to extend to Aldeburgh, a small harbour and fishing town. The line was opened on 12 August 1860. From GE to BR days the predominant locomotives on the line were J15 0–6–0s, and E4 2–4–0s. This photograph shows J15 No 65447 arriving at Aldeburgh station on 14 May 1956. On 10 June 1956 passenger services were taken over by dmus which operated a through service from Ipswich, unlike the steam services which originated from Saxmundham. Aldeburgh lost its goods services on 30 November 1959, only the impending construction of Sizewell Nuclear Power Station giving the line a five year reprieve. Despite various economies, including the use of conductor-guards, the line closed to passengers on 12 September 1966. Part has been retained to Leiston, but beyond, the track has gone. (*H. C. Casserley*)

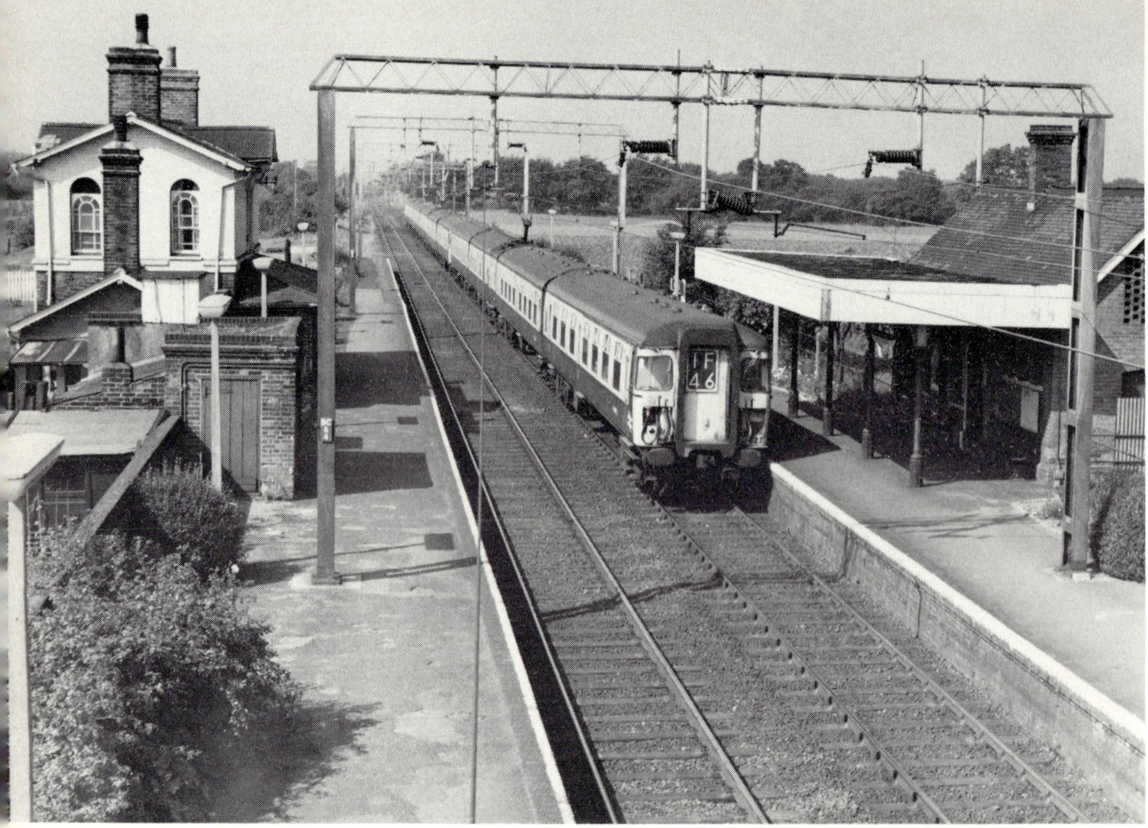
1F
46

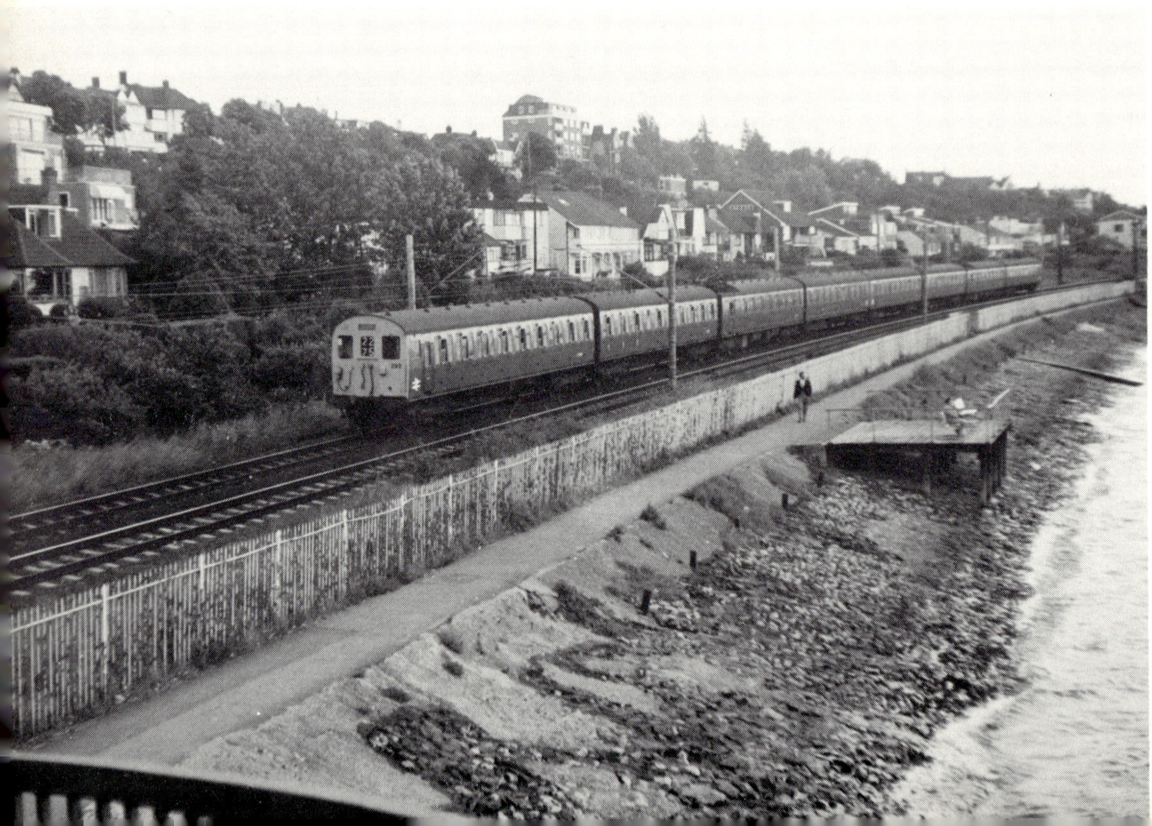

Top left: GE main line electrification in the early 1960s brought high voltage ac catenary between Liverpool Street and Colchester and to the Clacton and Walton-on-Naze branches. Through express services were turned over to electric multiple-unit four- and two-car sets with through gangways and open and side corridor layout internally. Here a 10-car formation passes Alresford in 1970. (*G. R. Mortimer*)

Left: The first world war prevented the Midland Railway's promised electrification of the LTSR line and times were not propitious for doing so after the Grouping. The long awaited event finally came in the early 1960s with the high voltage ac overhead system. In July 1974 a 1959-built eight-car formation of Class 302 units is seen on the sea front between Leigh-on-Sea and Chalkwell on a down Fenchurch Street–Shoeburyness working. (*T. Proctor*)

Above: A Class 37 English Electric Co-Co diesel passes Broxbourne with a Cambridge–Liverpool Street train in July 1980. (*M. L. Rogers*)

11. THE MODERN SCENE

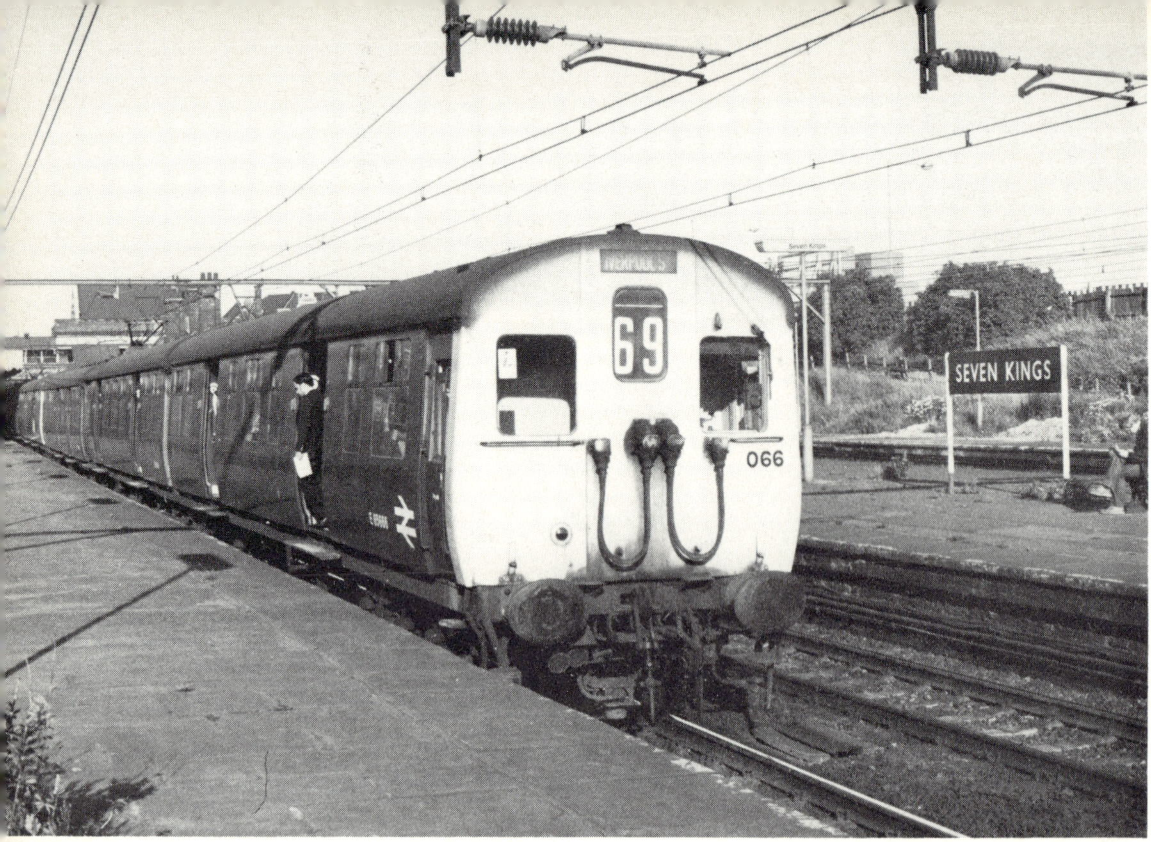
69
066
SEVEN KINGS

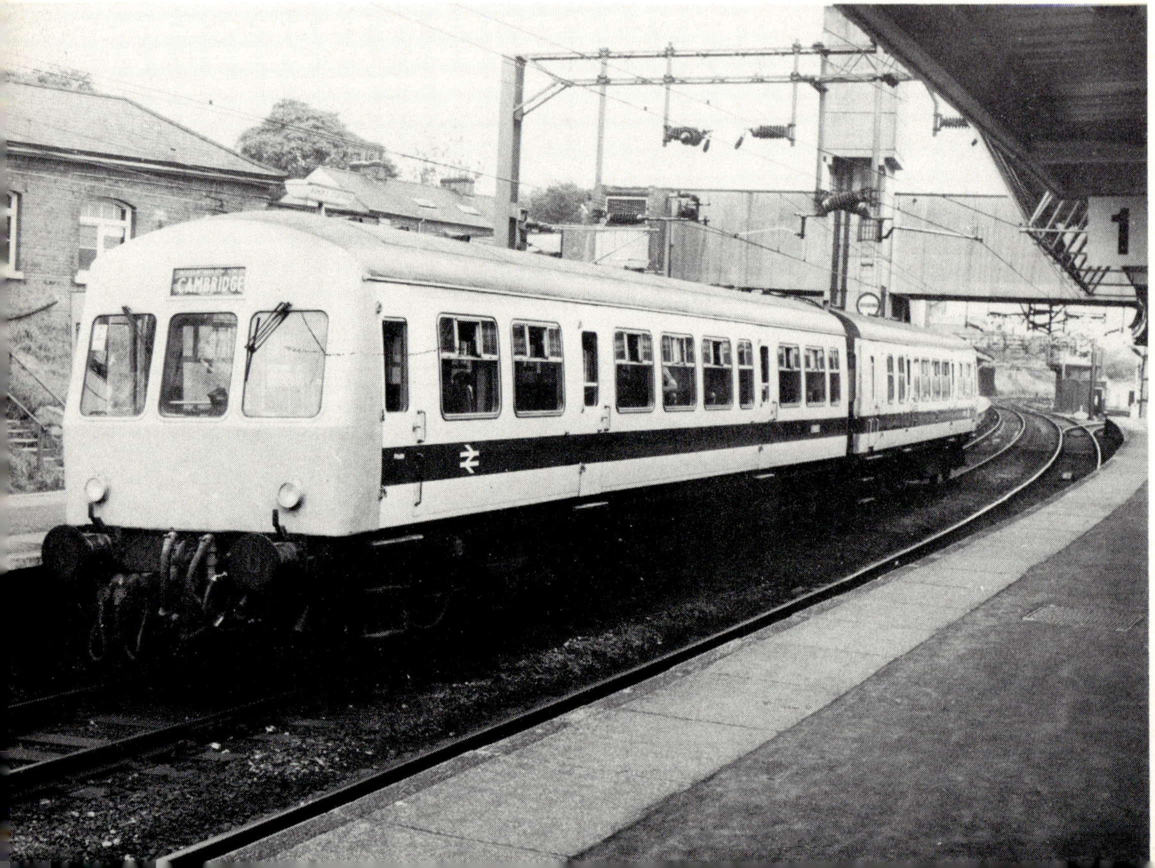
CAMBRIDGE
1

Top left: The original LNER-designed electric trains for the 1949 electrification between Liverpool Street and Shenfield were built for 1500V dc operation. In the early 1960s they were adapted for 6.25/25kV ac supplies through new transformer/rectifier equipment. Despite the destination indicator a nine-car train of three Class 306 units pauses at Seven Kings heading for Gidea Park in 1980. (*M. L. Rogers*)

Left: A refurbished Metro-Cammell two-car diesel multiple-unit waits to leave Bishops Stortford, the present end of electric services from London, on a stopping service to Cambridge. (*M. L. Rogers*)

Above: A Class 305 three-car suburban unit, newly liveried in blue and grey, leaves Broxbourne on a Hertford East-Liverpool Street service in 1980. (*M. L. Rogers*)

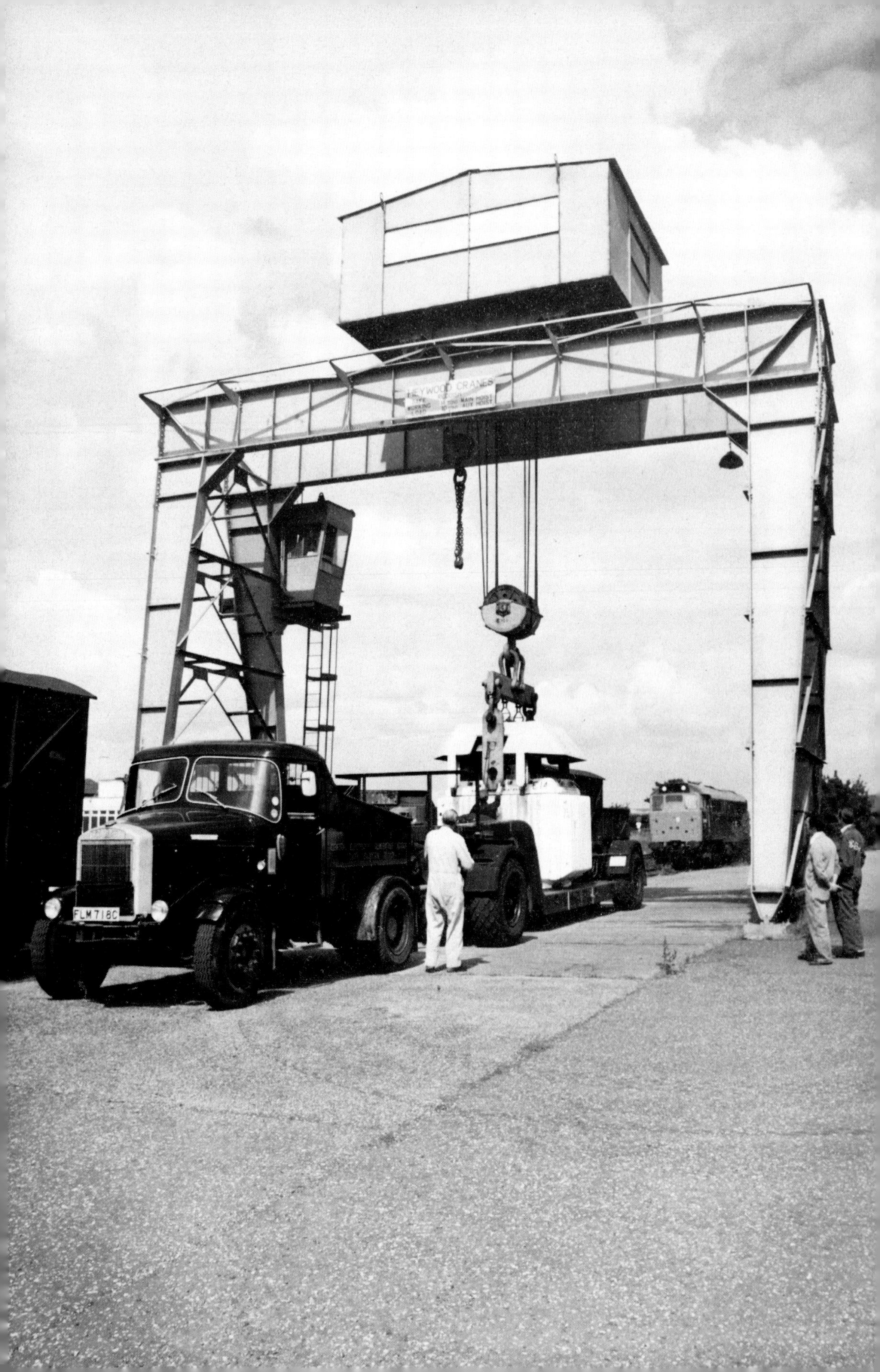
HEYWOOD CRANES
FLM 718C

12. PRESERVATION

Probably the most photographed locomotive in the world is Gresley A3 Pacific No 4472 *Flying Scotsman*. It was the last steam locomotive to work over Great Eastern metals before the 'Return to Steam' was allowed by BR. Here it is seen on the centre road at Ipswich on its last appearance in East Anglia, the date 17 May 1969. Note the Pullman car behind the tender. From here the train went forward to turn on Manningtree triangle. (*East Anglian Daily Times*)

Left: Part of the Aldeburgh branch is still used by trains carrying spent fuel from the Central Electricity Generating Board's 580 megawatt Magnox Sizewell A Reactor near Leiston. A flask of spent fuel is being lifted from a road carrier to a train for movement to Windscale in Cumbria. It is interesting to reflect that the branch exists today in the length envisaged by its planners 120 years ago but they would be amazed by the reason for its retention. (*CEGB*)

1N13
I'M GOING TO
GREENE KING
COUNTRY
Abbot Ale
GREENE KING
LONG VEHICLE
MVG 90H

SOUTHERN

Top left: A somewhat incongruous sight in East Anglia: in a layby south of Colchester on the main A12 road, an ex-Southern Railway Maunsell development of the Urie S15 4–6–0 reposes on a low loader towards the end of its journey from Dai Woodham's scrapyard at Barry to the Stour Valley Preservation Society at Chappel & Wakes Colne. The advertising material refers to the West Suffolk Brewery which sponsored the movement. In the background Class 47 No 1572, still in two-tone green livery, passes under the wires with a Norwich train for London. (*John Peachey*)

Left: After restoration the S15 resumed its Southern Railway identity as No 841 and was named *Greene King* after its sponsors. On 16 March 1975 the locomotive is seen giving yard rides at Chappel, wearing nameplates on the smoke deflectors. They were subsequently replaced by a pair above the centre driving wheels. By slewing the track No 841 was released from Chappel to work three main line excursions. Sadly it did not cover itself with glory on these occasions and was the last steam locomotive to work on East Anglian main lines. After spending a short period on the Nene Valley Railway *Greene King* is now on the North Yorkshire Moors Railway.

Above: Bressingham near Diss is justly famed as a steam Museum. It is also host to such famous locomotives as *Royal Scot, Duchess of Sutherland*, Holden J17 0–6–0 No 1217E, an ex-SNCF 141R 2–8–2 and a DB 2–10–0. There are also three different narrow gauge lines. In 1969 Norwegian Mogul No 377 came to Bressingham where it is seen in steam. During 377's sojourn in Norfolk it was repainted apple green and named *King Haakon VII*. It subsequently went to the Great Central Railway where it was one of the first steam locomotives to work at Loughborough. *King Haakon VII* returned to Bressingham on 21 April 1981.

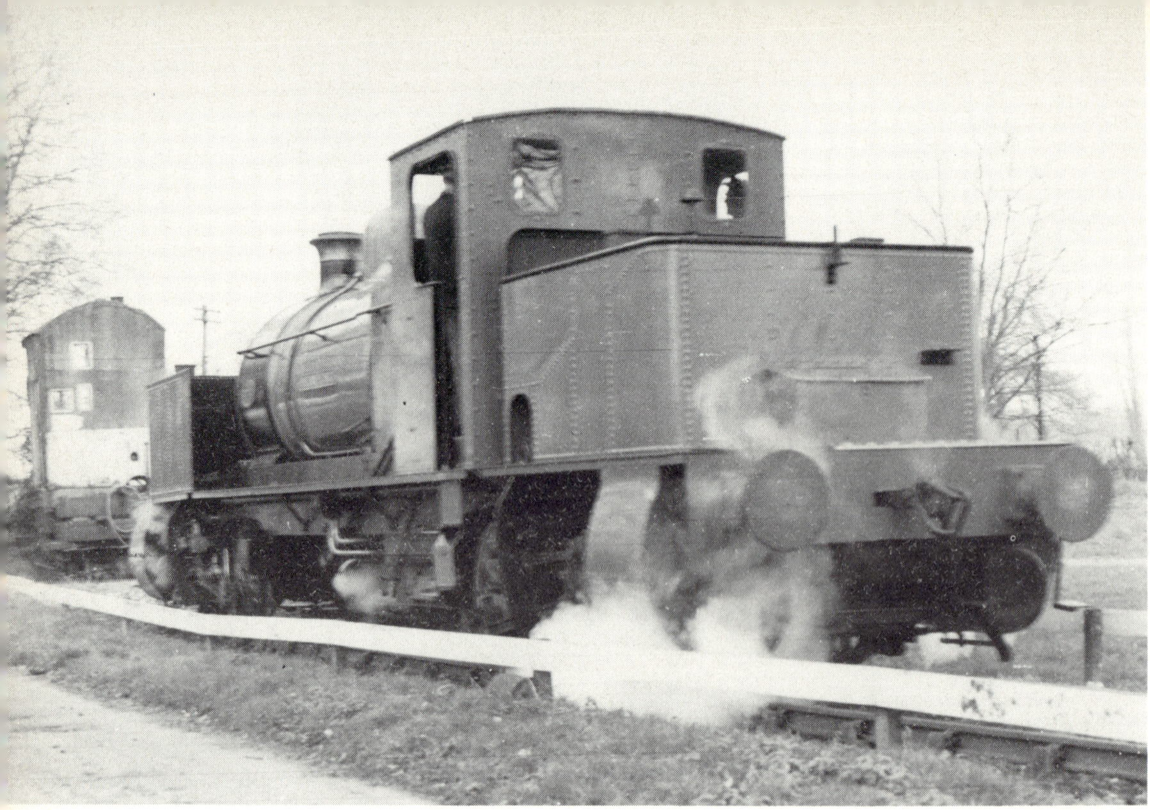

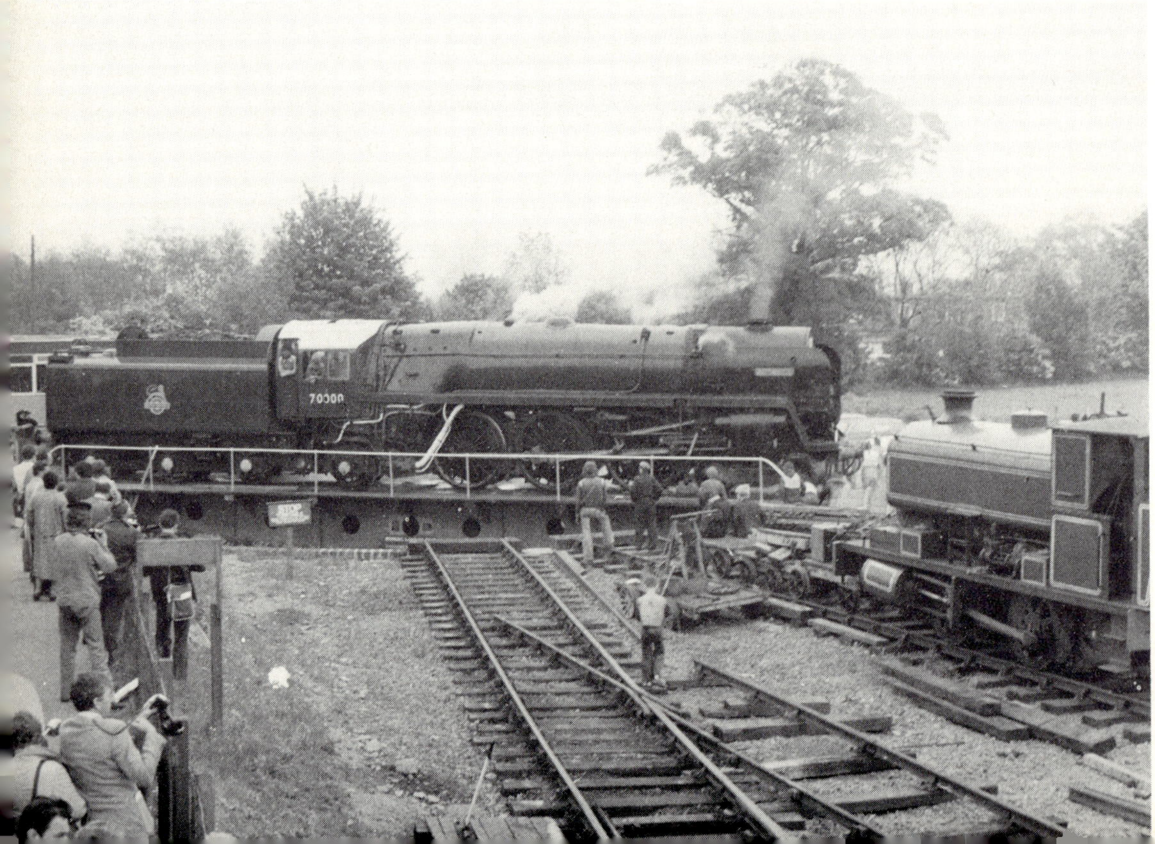
70000

Top left: Bressingham is also host to the only working Beyer-Garrett locomotive in the United Kingdom. This is the Ex-NCB Badesley Colliery 0–4–0 + 0–4–0 *William Francis* which is seen in steam in the mid 1970s.

Left: At Wansford adjacent to the A1 Great North Road, lies the headquarters of the Nene Valley Railway. This former London & North Western Railway line has been adapted to the 'Berne' continental loading gauge (about 1ft wider and higher than the BR profile) and it is possible to use Continental locomotives and rolling stock. An impressive collection of European stock has been assembled. From April 1980 the NVR has also been the home of the first BR Standard Pacific No 70000 *Britannia* which is seen on the turntable on 24 May 1980, the first time the engine had been turned in steam since withdrawal by BR.

Above: Sheringham station is the headquarters of the North Norfolk Railway which runs for some 5½ miles to Weybourne. At Easter 1977 Peckett 0–6–0ST No 5 waits at Sheringham to depart for Weybourne. The locomotive is finished in the M&GN colour of yellow ochre.

Overleaf: Typical of the Nene Valley Railway's collection of Continental engines are these ex-Swedish State Railways tanks. Class S 2–6–2T No 1178, built in 1914, and Class S1 2–6–4T No 1928, built 1953, head a train of Norwegian coaches across the River Nene at Ferry Meadows. (*John Titlow*)

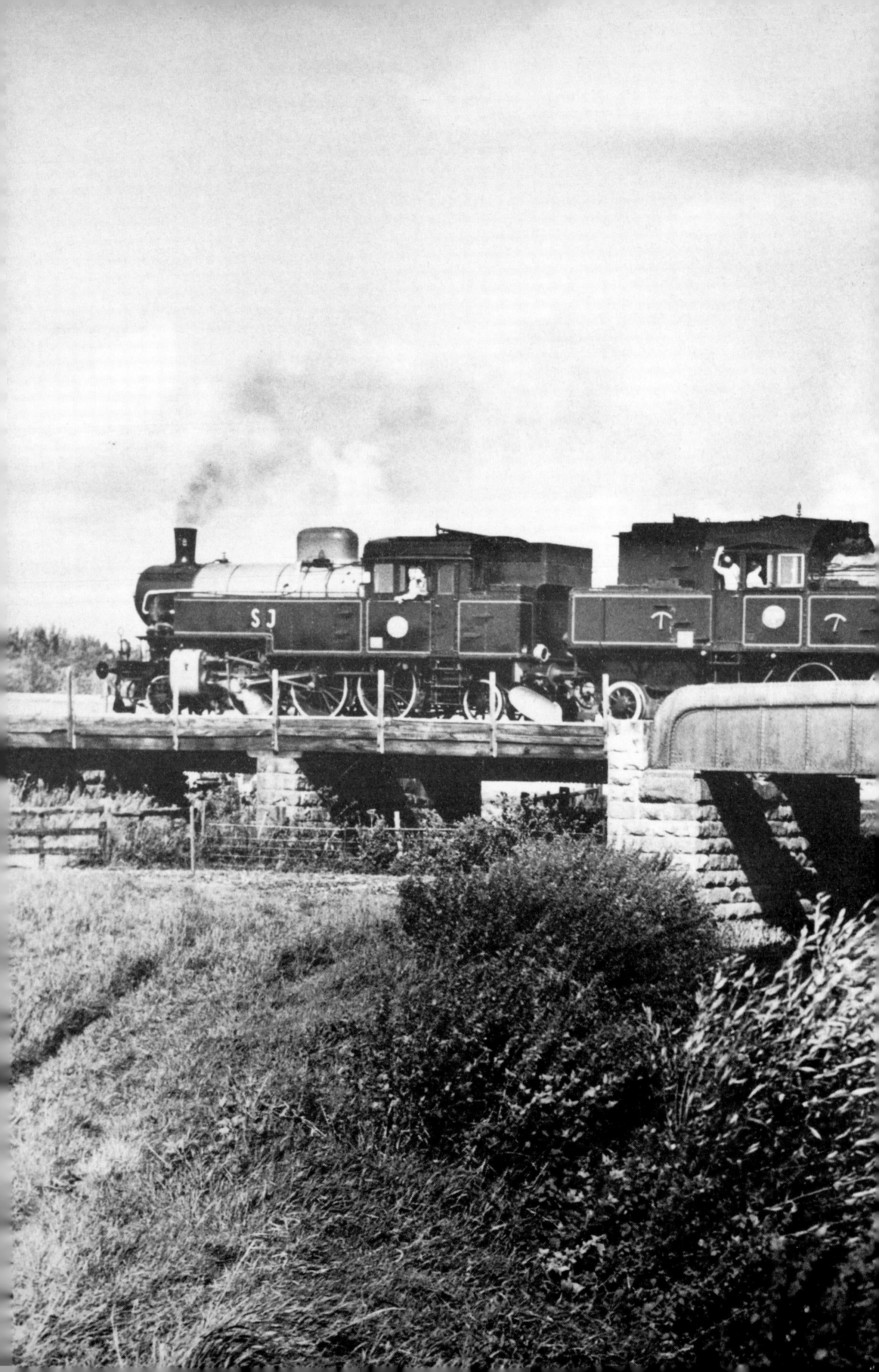
SJ

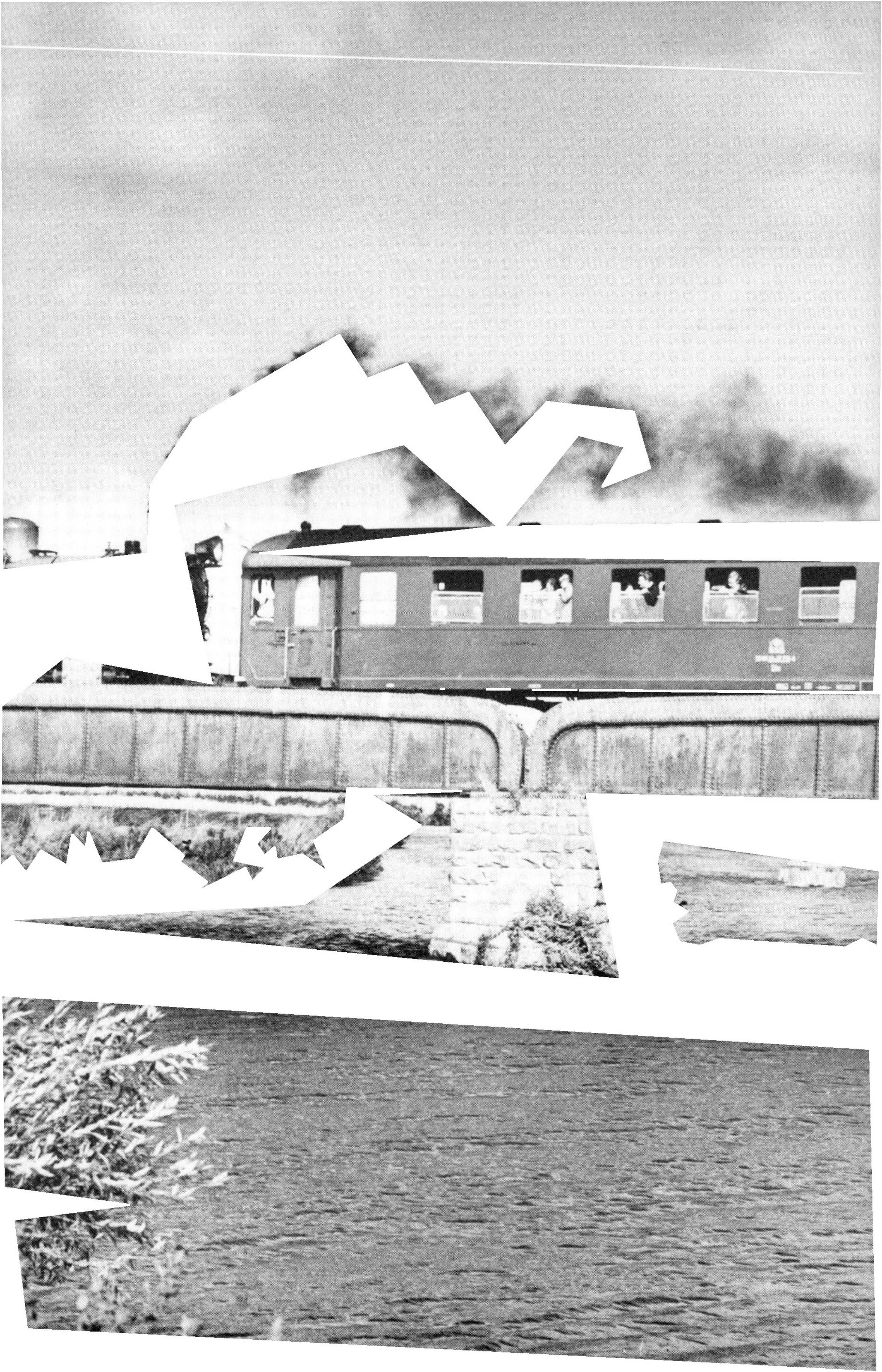

Gone but not totally forgotten – the sad remains of a B17. The nameplate of No 61639 *Norwich City* is mounted above the main gate of the football club after which the locomotive was named. It must have been some kick!